THE FIFTH MYSTIC REBEL

A Novel by
M. RASHEED

First published by Second Sight Graphix 2022

Copyright © 2022 by M. Rasheed

All rights reserved. No part of this publication may be reproduced, stored or transmitted in any form or by any means, electronic, mechanical, photocopying, recording, scanning, or otherwise without written permission from the publisher. It is illegal to copy this book, post it to a website, or distribute it by any other means without permission.

M. Rasheed has no responsibility for the persistence or accuracy of URLs for external or third-party Internet Websites referred to in this publication and does not guarantee that any content on such Websites is, or will remain, accurate or appropriate.

This novel is a work of fiction. Except for #ADOS, ADOS Advocacy Foundation, Yvette Carnell, Antonio Moore, BreakingBrown and tonetalks—whom the author wishes to promote and elevate—all other names, characters and incidents portrayed that drive the narrative are the caricatured inventions of the author's imagination. Any resemblance to actual persons, living or dead, events or localities is entirely coincidental.

Library of Congress Catalog Control Number: 2022906653

First edition

ISBN: 978-0-692-98222-8

This book was professionally typeset on Reedsy. Find out more at reedsy.com

For Antonio, Yvette &
the American Descendants of Slavery

Preface

My father shared his rare book list with me about a year and a half before he passed away in the spring of 2004.

Handwritten carefully with a golf pencil in his all-caps script, he held hope that I could help him track down a few of them as I was then in the habit of scouring the used book stores in the greater Detroit area to capture buried treasure from my own list. The recipient of several open-heart surgeries and progressively failing health, Dad was no longer able to keep up the hunt himself.

The first item I noticed was titled "The Circus of Dr. Lao" by Charles G. Finney. I remembered Dad being excited to catch the 1964 film adaptation of Finney's book, "The 7 Faces of Dr. Lao," when it showed on television several years before. Starring a heavily made-up Tony Randall as the mysterious titular character, and several other colorful figures besides, Dad showed particular fascination with Randall's depiction of Apollonius of Tyana, a contemporary of the Christ Jesus (*peace be upon him*). I assumed, as I read through Dad's list, that he wanted Finney's book to see if there were even more scenes featuring the ascetic philosopher within the heftier length novel. I was not wrong, as Dad was a fan of a least the fictionalized version of the legendary figure.

A few years later, after discovering the miraculous powers of the Internet, I would one-by-one inside of a year, track down and purchase every item on Dad's list – though by then he was sadly gone. I read his books myself, noticing with interest that the book Dad had titled "The Four Mystic Rebels" by Harry C. Schnur held an extensive biographical entry of Apollonius as the very first chapter. The book turned out to be more than a fun read for me, quickly becoming one of my favorites among my own personal influences, but there was a mystery. For all of my searching, I was never actually able to find "The Four Mystic Rebels." Instead, it appeared the only title was just "Mystic Rebels." At first, I thought that publishers had shortened the name with later editions, but no. The original 1949 monograph was named 'Mystic Rebels,' listing the four mystics as the subtitle. Why then did Dad call it "The Four Mystic Rebels?" I continued to call the book that myself, just because it was my beloved father's mysterious quirk.

Nearly a decade later, while reading Gerald Massey's "Egyptian Book of the Dead and the Ancient Mysteries of Amenta," I came across this mention:

> **The Real Gospel Jesus**
> After the Bishops of the Nicean Council had invented their Hesus Kristos, a search began for an ancient character of renown to play the part of an actual man on the stage of life. Who would he be? None other than Apollonius of Tyaneus, one of the Four Mystic Rebels listed in the work of Harry C. Schnur.

Mystery solved.

Obviously, it was Massey's enthusiastic and over-generous usage of capitalization that had caused the confusion. In any event, the 'damage' had been done. The son would willfully carry on the accidental tradition of the father – "The Four Mystic Rebels" will be the title of Schnur's book henceforth and forever more. At least within my own head, so that the title of this book you're reading will make sense.

As a quick aside, the inclusion of the above Massey quote does not mean I am partnered with him on that subject, since my belief system recognizes the literal "Real Gospel Jesus" as the very human Yeshua, son of Maryam, last anointed Hebrew messenger in the line of Isaac (*peace be upon the prophets of God!*)

According to Schnur, the reason why he chose these particular four personages to showcase, was because they alone of the numerous Western figures claiming wonder working/psychic abilities, were the only ones where the gift seemed legitimate. Described as minor occurrences that had even less effect on anything worthwhile, the second sight incidents stood out as much for their conspicuous lack of overblown pomp and fancy showmanship razzmatazz as the mystics themselves seemed disinclined to focus on them. This was especially interesting for a figure like Mystic Rebel #4 Joseph "Cagliostro" Balsamo, who built his entire career on the overblown pomp and fancy showmanship razzmatazz of the professional grifter commonplace during the height of the Age of the Magicians.

For my own purposes, having had two spiritual experiences known as the legendary "third eye" opening events back in the summer of 2018 – combined with my commitment to bitterly raw and cognitive dissonance inducing anti-racism art activism – I confidently proclaim that I, too, am a "mystic rebel" using Harry C. Schnur's strict criteria. I'll admit I lack even a fraction of the crowd-moving charisma of even the least of those four, but it is of no matter. What I can do is use my art (here I speak of the novel you are currently reading, as you hope that I finally manage to cut off this rambling preface so you can get to it) to fictionalize my humble personal spiritual concepts into something more fun & interesting for an art platform such as a novel, combined with an awareness message for the potency of the much needed #ADOS movement that the Black American former slave class absolutely needs to suffuse into their long-dormant political muscles, transformed into a grand narrative capable of touching hearts and minds on at least a small scale. Is this not my job as the artist?

So, I thank the One God for the energy and inspiration to produce a novel, as well as shout out a special thanks to my late father for initiating this journey by trusting me with his precious book list. Let us get to it.

Muhammad Rasheed
21 Mar 2022
mrasheed.com

1

PROLOGUE

"Oh, my God! It is happening! It's happening again!"

Malang Flathill sat up straight in the wooden kitchen chair as his viewpoint shifted in an instant from the mundane (modest kitchen with pastel green tiled walls, wooden table, stainless-steel gas stove and matching stainless-steel refrigerator), to the fantastic.

A vast, endless wall made up of some kind of quasi-transparent foam stood seemingly six inches away from Malang's voracious stare. His eyes felt as large as dinner plates! It felt like he was SEEING with all of his senses at once, as if this mysterious second sight into another world was tasked with extra duty to make up for the other senses as well as its own vision job. Malang was still conscious of the tingling energized sensation that had gradually taken over his being until this happened – another 'third eye' vision! The second in two weeks!

Like the last time, Malang didn't spend too much time studying the odd, membranous wall. Within it, at just above brow height, was another fist-sized portal, the edges composed of more densely-packed bubbles of the wall's foam, slowly swirling around the brightly glowing "Wisdom Eye." The imagery within the 'third eye' portal was different this time though. Malang was conscious of the bliss he was feeling during this experience, conscious of the limited amount of time he had to visually record all that was shown to him since the exhilarating sensation of tingling energy that suffused his entire body—the Serpent Fire of the Universe—was clearly marking a countdown in its rapid dissipation.

Malang directed his full focus into the "third eye" portal. The preternaturally crystal-clear vision within was of a burning building that he had never seen before. A Southern plantation 'big house' style dwelling, not in disrepair as he would expect such a building to be in the modern day, but in good shape, until the flames licked the paint as he watched and turned it into anything but. The "third eye" directed the view of Malang's conscious vision, spinning him around the big house, zooming in closer to areas it appeared to want him to view with concentrated scrutiny. Malang obliged, taking in every detail his disembodied consciousness could see. The "third eye" zoomed out showing one more view of the front of the building just as the Serpent Fire of the Universe depleted and his vision returned to the green-tiled kitchen of his home on the east side of Chocolate City, Mishigamaa.

His mind raced as he reviewed both the event of this second "third eye" experience, as well as the details of the imagery shown, over and over again. Outside of the fantastic nature of the event itself, Malang found himself greatly moved and thankful. The exhilaration mimicked what he felt after the last event two weeks ago, but it didn't take long for doubt to creep in ("Did I really see what I thought I saw…?") and the last few days found him ready to abandon the whole thing as a weird mind fart. A mistake.

It was no mistake.

Malang Flathill ("ME!") was blessed with two ("TWO!!") bona fide, rare spiritual signs known by the Ancient Egyptians as the UDJAT Eye of Heru – the Wisdom Eye of Second Sight. It was clear that the second one, outside of whatever was shown to him in the portal itself, functioned as a confirmation and a comfort to ease his mind and soul... he saw what he saw... a true glimpse into the unseen spirit. There was no need to doubt.

Malang took a sip of his coffee, half surprised it was still hot after what seemed like a lifetime of excitement had just occurred, stood and walked into the living room to pace while he gathered his thoughts. A silvery gray couch sat against the wall opposite the front door, a four-paned picture window behind it showed the view of the neighbors' homes beyond. A large oriental rug covered the floor and Malang traced a path – placing one foot just before the other – from one side of the room to the next as he continued to review the event.

Honestly, why should he doubt? Approximately three years before, Malang had found himself personally confronted by the Lord's offer of the Ultimate Reward of paradise's eternal bliss in exchange for "a beautiful loan" as revealed in the 245th verse of the Qur'an's second chapter. Meaning, that God was telling the believer to trust the Divine, do as we were commanded by refraining from wrongdoing, doing what was right, and we would receive a wonderful life that would LAST... a spiritual life of unimaginable wonders brought to us by the same Supreme Creator who provided everything that we've come to love in this lesser, finite material realm of illusion. As an accomplished, award-winning genre creator (Shargayt the Seawolf comics! Collect 'em all!) Malang decided to put his imagination on that idea and really meditate upon it. Instead of the typical seeing the topic from the pop cultural idea of "heaven" – commonly caricatured by gag cartoonists and comedy sketch shows – Malang pragmatically asked himself what would it truly mean if the Supreme Creator of the universe gifted him with an everlasting "Ultimate Reward" that he currently could not even imagine? Would such a thing be worth sacrificing for?

He decided that it would be.

Malang rededicated himself to his religion of Al-Islam with a renewed vigor, actioning concepts and rituals he was previously merely walking through. Of special note was God's command: *"Seek help with prayer and patient perseverance, for the One God is with those who patiently persevere."* The precise wording caught Malang's attention this time. The One God says He's closer to the believer when we are practicing fortitude during hardship than He is when we are praying. A powerful concept! Malang decided to build that "patient perseverance" principle into his lifestyle and accept God's beautiful loan offer at a deeper level.

He chose a worthy cause – anti-racism activism on behalf of his own much maligned Black American ethnic group – and built his art around it in an art activist structure. Committed to producing gripping awareness pieces that struck right to the heart of the issue (feelings be damned), Malang put himself on a schedule that would challenge him around the clock, triggering the need to continuously encourage himself not to give up. It seemed like a good idea, but he felt a pang of doubt; he'd be lying if he didn't admit there was a certain amount of self-indulgence involved. Malang was a trained artist, after-all. He loved to create anyway. Even though this new artivism spiritual path FELT right from the logic of it he worked out, how could he know that it was really right and accepted by the One God?

It was right on the heels of the height of this nagging doubt that he experienced his first "third eye" event, the Wisdom Eye revealing imagery that left no doubt at all that Malang's artivism idea dedicated to God's beautiful loan call was indeed the Right Path for him.

The phone rang just as Malang reached the end of the rug as he paced, pivoting on his heel to retrace his steps. He broke stride to dart into the bedroom, picking up his red-cased cell to answer his wife.

"Hi, bae!"

"Hi, sleepyhead! How's your day off?"

"It's great. I have a thing," said Malang with an

unconscious cheesy grin. "How are you two doing? Is Livvy enjoying her relatives?"

"Yes, chile. My mom is spoiling her right now, feeding her off her plate. We're out here on the porch – Me, Olivia, Mom and your crazy brother-in-law. Mom said, 'Hi,' Malang. Everyone says… Malang said, 'Hello!' We're good. You said you're having a great time on your off?"

"Margaret, it happened AGAIN! I had another 'third eye' opening event not even thirty minutes ago!"

"What?! Oh, my God! That is great. How do you feel?" Margaret asked warily. Malang caught the caution in her voice, but ignored it. He was already in the habit, during these past two weeks, of being protective of the experiences from any kind of nay saying negativity from wheresoever it may come, even from her. It was his own treacherous mind that needed to be tamed in the end and Malang was determined that a miraculous second "third eye" opening would be the cure he needed from any internal doubts. He didn't even ask for a sign from God as evidence that the first event was real (Malang was too knowledgeable of scripture to perform that foolishness), but it was gifted to him anyway. He would not be one to squander a gift from heaven; he felt immensely grateful.

"I still feel exhilarated from it," he said. "I feel

energized and like I can do anything! I have the tangible feeling that my Lord has my back and I can't lose. That how I feel." Malang went on to describe it in detail—the event itself as well as the burning house imagery shown to him.

"I think I should write about it, Margaret. On my blog. I don't want to tell them what I saw, the customized vision within the 'third eye' is just for me. I'm sure of that. It's the actual experience of the portal openings that happened around what was shown that is a universal spiritual event that I think I need to chronicle for the human record. I think we all should immediately write out our glimpses into the unseen spirit and have them available for public study. Talking about that stuff candidly is the only way we can really study that side of our human existence, right?"

"Well, I guess," said Margaret with a doubting tone dragging the syllable out. "Maybe you should just write it out for yourself in a private personal journal though, do you think?"

"If I don't courageously put it out there, how will I be able to speak with people who also had the same thing happen to them?"

"Remember, I, too, had visions!" she practically blurted. "They were clearly not 'just' dreams."

"I know they were not just conventional dreams; they were prophetic and were definitely spirit visions," said Malang, putting his coffee cup in the microwave. "Did you see a glowing round hole, approximately six inches in front of your face, that the visions were shown to you through?"

"No."

"Then they were spiritual visions, but they weren't 'third eye' opening visions. That manifested glowing round portal framing the vision is the signature sign of the Wisdom Eye of legend, but most people don't know about it and wouldn't know if it happened to them. I need to blog about this. We all should. It's important."

2

All That Talkin'

A little under 300,000 participants enthusiastically converged upon the 39th Annual Chocolate City Jazz Festival at the historic Heath Galleria.

Featuring an assortment of live performing artists such as Herbie Hancock, Mavis Staples, Otis Clay, Bettye Lavette, The Miracles, Curtis Fuller and Gerald Wilson, with endless vendors and great food, the four decades old Labor Day weekend tradition certainly lived up to its reputation.

For about a month and a half now, Malang Flathill had been seeking out opportunities to display his politically-charged paintings wherever he could find a suitable crowd of Black Americans to see them and engage. With little interest in actually selling the pieces, he was primarily focused on expressing the economic empowerment concepts they were inspired by for his people's awareness. The passersby on the impressively-crowded jazz festival walkway were game enough, possessed of just the right amount of art appreciation and an ear for an invigorating word from a passionate speaker, it didn't take Malang long to gather a decent group of curious listeners shortly after he first set up his booth. Standing at five feet, 10 inches tall, with a medium build and sporting a short fade with not quite even amounts of black & grey, Malang wore loose-fit black cargo pants, a grey long-sleeve t-shirt and tan loafers, as he gestured at the 20 prints displayed. Each showcased anti-racism, pro-Black American economic empowerment themes in his signature cartoony illustrative art style. His eyes flashed as he made his points in the heat of his passion for the topic.

"Remember the 1972 Gary, Indiana Black Political Convention?" Malang asked, pushing his sleeves up to the elbow. "Realistically, it could be considered the end cap of the civil rights movement. Still grieving from the aftermath of Hoover's 'Black messiah' assassination protocols that left Dr. King, Malcolm, Hampton and many others slain or imprisoned, the remaining second and third tier leaders, to their credit, decided correctly that they should fight to implement the logical next steps taking advantage of the 1964 Civil Rights and 1965 Voting Rights Acts. They realized that the practical application of those Acts was 1.) a Black Political Agenda with a list of bullets that would lead to our long-withheld Reparations and economic inclusion into a protected wealth building ownership class, and 2.) the hand-groomed, elected, dedicated political representation who would fight for that Black Political Agenda at every stage of the U.S. government. This is exactly what the Black American needs—then as now—to come together as a focused special interest bloc to fight for what we are owed as the builders of the wealthiest nation on earth."

"To you."

Malang looked over in the direction of the defiant comment. In his heart of hearts, he genuinely hoped it had been uttered by a white person, so that he could at least smirk and sarcastically snap at the typical snark he reasonably expected from his classic ideological foe, but no. It was a light-skinned Black man, tanned a golden-red after clearly enjoying the summer outdoors. He was shaved bald with a gleaming diamond in his left ear, his head tilted to his left with a cynical twisted lip. "Yes, it is so to me, since the narrative is coming from research into the factual events of history. If you doubt me, you can always just look it up; the 1972 National Black Political Convention is not a secret. I would expect it to likewise reflect your own opinion, too, unless you are committed to being perverse for no reason."

"Man, nobody even wants to hear all of that, dawg. See, blackies[1] like y'all just want us to play

---

[1] I've decided not to use the [n-word] at all in this book. When you, Dear Reader, see "blackie," that's what it means, carrying over from how I've been dealing with it in my editorial cartoons. FYI. ~MR

victim all the time. We will never get ahead because white folks won't want to work with that shit!"

"You're saying that instead of using the political tools put in place on our behalf by our slain civil rights leaders, we should instead abandon the struggle all together so that—instead of getting our own rightful piece of the United States of America's wealth & resource we are owed – we should be happy with a position white people give some of us inside of their white-owned monopolies, and don't make them uncomfortable by protesting their foul, racist treatment."

"I didn't say all of that," the bald guy said dismissively. "Now you puttin' words in my mouth."

Malang allowed a brief chuckle to escape him. "Okay, so tell me what you actually meant then. From my point of view, I have nowhere else to go in interpreting your comment. You don't like to hear people… BLACK people… discussing where we went wrong, what we did right and theorizing on what we need to do to get back on the path towards achieving our full birthright freedoms as American citizens. You hate it on behalf of the angry racist white pay-masters. Is that not an accurate reflection of what you MEANT?"

"It's not just all black & white though! Crying 'racism' this and 'racism' that ain't all there is! What about our own responsibility in everything? All of our problems ain't white people shit, it's OUR shit!" The bald guy pounded his chest with an open right hand for dramatic effect to receive some approval from the crowd.

"Our own responsibility is exactly what I'm talking about. Did I not mention 'political tools?' The principle of 'the squeaky wheel gets the grease' is what politics is all about. The government's massive spending power has never been leveraged in the direction of the Black American former slave class with any meaningful intent, other than to do us wrong, like the birth of the expressway system and how those highways were deliberately run through Black business districts to economically elevate others by hurting us. This happens precisely because we are disenfranchised – 30 million scattered, weakly self-interested individualists within the 'crabs-in-a-barrel' trap of the Assimilated Integrationist Token era. It would not happen if we were unified in a political identity GROUP self-interest, using our collective force like a scalpel to carve out our needs from our government's innards. Playing the game correctly with focused determination and fortitude, while looking out for each other as if we are all we have (because we are!) is how we can finally win."

"Maaaaan, just because YOU ain't winning—-!"

"I'm not talking about me," Malang interrupted.

"Politics isn't about me as the individual, it's about the economic uplift of the group."

"Yeah, right. You ain't sold one of those lame-assed prints yet. Look at all these people. Blackie, you WACK." The bald guy walked away with a sneer. Malang looked after him, trying to resist the urge to show irritation on his face, or even to shake his head in annoyed disappointment with his people when they act like that. Hearing white supremacist talking points ("playing victim") spewed at him from Black American faces is a bit much, despite knowing the multi-tentacled history of why they would do it. Knowing the why doesn't lessen the sting of being an eye-witness to his own ethnic group being willfully foolish for no other reason than they fear they won't make it in life without kowtowing to 'whiteness' in some way. He needed to express to them they would fare better to move forward in their strength, not stay moving backwards in weakness. Either way it's going to be hard, so why not choose the harder path of the two with the greatest reward on the other side? To Malang it made perfect sense; he reached for his notepad as this line of thought inspired an idea for a painting.

"What's your name, young blood?"

"I'm Malang, sir. Yours?"

"Frank. I'm please to meet you. You're doing

good work here."

"Thank you!" said Malang, initiating a firm, respectful handshake. "I appreciate you saying so."

"Naw, thank you, Malang. I was listening to your discussion with the other cat. Y'know, I was at that Gary Convention back in 1972. You brought back a lot of really intense memories… I started to say, 'great memories,' but where did all of our good work go after that historic weekend? Like you said it was a great plan, so why are we in worst shape as a people *TODAY!* than we were back then?"

Malang studied the older gentleman. He was dark-skinned and slender. Hunched forward, he gave the illusion of being shorter than Malang, but that was not likely true. He was clean shaven and also bald, a gold ring tugged down on his right earlobe, with a navy-blue ball cap sporting a golf tournament logo perched on his head. He wore crisp light jeans, an off-white Members Only jacket and black sneakers. "Honestly," Malang said carefully. "It wasn't likely that the same people who killed Malcolm X and Dr. King would allow the two's organizational heirs to successfully carry on their work without a fight. And the bad guys fight dirty."

"You right about that!" said Frank.

"Call to mind the special restrictions that the 1972 Gary Convention operated under. They refused to allow white people or the white-owned press inside. One notable Black organization refused to participate for that very reason, and made a show of having very vocal members milling around outside talkin' mess. Do you remember who that was?"

Frank furrowed his brow and looked up at a turkey leg booth's signage to his right. "Y'know, I can't say that I remember that."

"It was the NAACP," said Malang in a dramatic tone.

"DAMN!"

"Oh, it gets worse. The convention leaders determined that their priorities were two-fold as I mentioned. First, saturate the U.S. government with fiercely loyal Black elected officials, each religiously fighting for our Black Political Agenda. They determined that the convention would not end without finalizing that Agenda. To their credit they successfully pulled that off."

"What? Well, where did…?"

"The NAACP stepped up and said they would take over from there and make sure it was properly distributed to the people. Over the next decade, legions of 'the first Black' something or another of politicians did indeed saturate the halls of American politics in record-breaking numbers. Conspicuously absent from their tool kit was the Black

Political Agenda which had vanished. Without that guidance from the voice of the Black American constituency to direct their platforms and work, whose political agenda have all of these Black politicians been fighting for in the last 50 years?"

"It couldn't have been us!" said Frank, his mouth twisted into a sneer as he slowly shook his head.

"No, indeed. Without that clear guidance from the people to hold them accountable, the Black politician became a tokenized careerist working for the partisan parties themselves, their activities impotent in liberating their own identity group from the devastating effects of centuries of accrued discrimination and plunder. However, our rivals benefited from their efforts greatly."

"Man, you ain't never lied!" Frank reached forward to give some dap. "Listen, Malang, it's been a real pleasure! You're making all these folks THINK! You keep going with it now. I'm gonna go on ahead and finish this row, get me something to eat."

"Thank you so much for your kind words. Take care."

Most of the group who had stayed to listen to the dialogue with the light-skinned guy had moved on. About eight people stayed to study Malang's prints, which included a Black father who appeared to be having a 'teachable moment' with a biracial young boy, a middle-aged Black woman in elaborately decorated glasses who already held several trinkets & knickknacks she had purchased, a tall, thin white man who stood back-a-ways with his hands behind his back, and a figure wearing a dashiki print tunic. This last caught Malang's eye and quickly looked away, moving on to look at another print. Malang had already met this guy, who also wore a black kufi cap sitting on short-cropped hair. A coffee-colored medium brown, similar to Malang's own tones, in linen pants and raw leather sandals, he manned an afrocentric-themed booth not too much further up the row. The two had held the gate open for one another several times as they brought in their equipment from the parking lot early that morning. Malang debated whether he should approach and solicit Dashiki guy's opinion to kick start a discussion, when the guy frowned. The print the guy was looking at was facing away, but Malang didn't need to see it; he knew what it depicted. Featuring a group of multi-ethnic Black African and Caribbean immigrants – each proudly sporting their national flag – while collectively berating a Black American figure for demonstrating equal pride in flying his own national colors of Old Glory. Malang briefly teased his memory for the full title of the piece ("Pan-African grifters continue the anti-Black American peculiar discrimination on behalf of white racist" or something like that) when Dashiki guy turned abruptly to walk back to his booth.

He'll be alright, Malang thought confidently. Give him some time to gather his thoughts and he'll be ready to discuss it.

Malang scanned the remaining window shoppers. The white guy with his hands behind his back was gone. The trinkets lady with the glasses was gone, no doubt over-burdened by the weight of her loot. Perhaps she had just gone to put her stuff in the car and would also be back. The Black father guy was still "kickin' knowledge" to the biracial kid. Malang was tempted to get closer to hear, but he didn't want to create an unwanted intrusion upon their moment. Surely, if the guy needed his input, he would simply ask.

"Excuse me, sir?"

Startled, Malang turned to find the lady with the bedazzled glasses and holding all the bags of purchased stuff. He noticed a new bag of items was added to her haul, picked up from the musical-themed snow-globe booth to his left. "Yes, ma'am! How may I help you?"

"Are you the artist, or are you just selling the prints?"

"Ah. I'm doing both." She inquired about the medium used and the price. Malang answered to her apparent satisfaction and she looked over the group of prints again with a sweeping eye.

"Do you have any about 'Black Girl Magic?' I'd like to see those."

"I do, but I didn't bring them today. I'll make sure to have them with me tomorrow, God willing." She thanked him, lingered a bit longer and then moved on down the row. Malang absently wondered if she was a hoarder.

He then focused his attention on a medium light-skinned Black man who was intensively studying a print that critiqued the Black Republican figure as a stereotype. The gentleman's arms were crossed over his long-sleeved, white dress shirt. He wore tan khakis and brownish-grey leather shoes. His hair was closely cropped, not quite bald. A diamond stud gleamed in his right ear. He seemed to look up to meet Malang's eye as soon as he was noticed. Malang stepped forward with a grin. "It would appear that the piece has given you a lot to ponder, yes?" The gentleman smiled, shaking his head.

"Well, that's one way to put it. The first thing I guess I need to ask – before I jump to any possibly unfair conclusions – is what is it actually intended to mean?"

"To put it as unambiguously as possible," said Malang, searching the guy's face for possible tells.

"The Black Republican of the modern era has decided that his ethnic group is not worth fighting for and he will instead 'get his' and work only on his own personal economic come up. The white-ran Republican Party itself will welcome such an attitude with open arms since, of course, the Black Republican isn't using his talents to uplift his group, he would be obliged to become a support class to his group's political rivals & enemies, in exchange for a little money."

"That's quite a bit to unpack."

"Is it? From my viewpoint, it's just a small piece within the greater mosaic of anti-racism scholarship. In fact, I think the precise relationship between the Black Republican to his people and the white racist aristocracy is the oldest and simplest one."

"And what relationship is that exactly?" asked the gentleman.

"The self-interested traitor."

"Wow."

"How else would I interpret what comes down to a 'if you can't beat em, join 'em' mindset?"

"You realize that… I'm sorry, what's your name?"

"Malang."

"Pleased to meet you, Malang. I'm John. You do realize that the Republican Party is the party of Abraham Lincoln and Frederick Douglass, don't you?"

"I do realize that," said Malang with a chuckle. "That's why I very carefully said 'The Black Republican of the modern era' when I began."

"So, you think this isn't the same Republican Party?"

"Why would it be? You yourself just pointed out that Frederick Douglass, who fought for the emancipation of his people before the Civil War and for their economic inclusion after it, was a Republican in his day. Does fighting for Reparations and economic inclusion for the Black American former slave class group sound like any modern Black Republican you know of?"

"I think that you're really asking the wrong question. What we should be asking today is whether the fight is really about racism anymore. Does it really make sense for us to be stuck in a mode of thinking from the 1960s? Racism, Malang? Really? We've gotten pass all of that."

"Okay, now it's my turn to shake my head in bafflement." Malang demonstrated to share a quick laugh between them. "So, you think that racism is over? That it was cured when, what? When the 1964 Civil Rights Act was signed?"

"I'm saying that the heavy-lifting on that work has already been done. During the Civil Rights Era, our leaders talked about race all the time *ad nauseam* – it was in every single media outlet for over a decade! They established affirmative action, scholarships, Black people assimilating into the national fabric in ways that were unprecedented up to that point. So, for me as a Black Republican to choose to be self-interested and join the party who most closely reflects my family's and my personal values, what's wrong with that?" John stepped back and tilted his head, inviting the counter.

"What's wrong with that mindset is that it seems to have only given a brief glimpse at the history of the Black American and our relationship to our country, and more importantly, our relationship to our political identity group rivals. That mindset seems to have been in such a hurry to pursue a self-interested lifestyle that it was all too eager to pick up conformation biased opinions and talking points about American racism to justify that horse-blinder self-interest. The fact that affirmative action didn't at all do what it was designed to do—which was to provide a program to get the poorest Black Americans job experience in white-owned businesses—but was changed just to meet quotas that turned into giving economic come ups to everyone except the original target group, is the perfect case in point. You used it to point out that racism has been mostly fixed, but it turns out, affirmative action was part of a folio of actions designed to neutralize the promise of the 1964 Civil Rights and 1965 Voting Rights Acts to keep Black Americans locked out of access as a group."

"Okay, well, look, " said John, his face flushed. "If we can agree that Black Americans are a small part of the national populace, and certain professions have low numbers of Black people in them, can we really consider that to be 'racism?'"

"Sure, we can!"

"What? How can you say that?"

"Okay, let's look at the 1866 Civil Rights Act – a robust law that gave the recently freed Black Americans the same rights to do business, establish companies, make contracts, receive lucrative government contracts – in short, do everything that our white counterparts can do to build wealth in the ownership class. That law functions under the assumption that there would be a competitive open free market to do business in. Instead, what we have are closed markets monopolized by powerful, white-owned, mega-corporate entities. With no room in those monopolized industries to compete fairly alongside whites as economic equals, we are forced to play their games and pretend that job slots within those monopolies complies to the letter and spirit of the 1866 Civil Rights Act. So, more Black doctors inside of white-dominated medical industry companies is not the same at all as Black-owned hospitals and medical research facilities that compete with white-owned hospitals and medical research facilities within those markets. Being a minuscule cog within someone's wealth-building machine is very different than competing eye-to-eye with a wealth-building ownership peer, right?"

"I'll give you that."

"Our people don't have that, John. We're locked out of access to the wealth-building ownership class we deserve to be in, but somehow you believe the racism work is behind us while you ran off to make a piece of money being a stooge for the white Republicans."

"Now you're going too far," John bristled.

"Is it too far?" asked Malang. "Is it not the truth?"

"We're 'locked out of access,' as you say by stubborn choice! By resisting Integration—which comes with financial success and psychological well-being—in favor of holding onto a poverty mentality of 'victimhood' associated with the leftist cultivated ghettoes, we've chosen to be on the outside! And for what? To hold onto a 'cultural blackness' that does not serve us. The idea is absurd. Racism isn't our problem; sabotaging ourselves within a self-inflicted cult of victimology is our problem."

"So, even though you responded, 'I'll give you that' to my pointing out that the goal of the 1866

Civil Rights Act was sabotaged by the architects of systemic racism to replace Black Americans becoming competitive economic equals in the wealth-building ownership markets with 'Assimilated Integrationist Tokens' within white-owned monopolies, you didn't actually 'give me that.' You immediately returned to treating being an employee in a white-owned monopolist corporation as the end of racism."

"Well…" John sputtered.

"Being an employee in someone else's company is not the same as having access to the capital, credit and enormous spending power of the U.S. government used to build wealth, John. Calling out that deliberate bait-n-switch and not merely surrendering into it doesn't mean I'm sabotaging my life. It means, as a rightful American citizen, that I demand what I am entitled to – full freedoms as promised me by the laws of the land."

"No one owes…"

"STOP!" shouted Malang. "I am indeed owed Reparations and economic inclusion by my ever-complicit government for the exploitation & plunder inflicted upon my group for centuries. That's why I'm poor as a group. Not because I refused to accept the substitute fake 'freedom' white people are offering, instead of the true freedoms promised me by the laws passed on my behalf."

"I don't think it's necessary for you to raise your voice like that. Up until now I thought you wanted a civil discussion, not a shouting match. I'm going to go ahead and leave. Good luck with your booth or whatever. Good bye."

John briskly walked away, his long stride quickly taking him out of sight. Malang felt his heart still beating loudly in his ears, his irritation at the "Integration" rhetoric spin job manifest. He didn't intend to get upset, but he would readily admit that John pressed a pet peeve button. To admit in one breath that the history of our people being locked out of access is a true statement, but then spin around to double-down on the ideological 'Integration' systemic racism bamboozle as a solution and blame us for rejecting a system designed to keep us as second tiered support class under 'whiteness' is infuriating. Especially for one 'awakened' to the fact that there is a world of difference between the empowered "economic inclusion" versus the leftist bait-n-switch concept of the modern "integration" slave state. If the opponent is just going to use the flash of rage at their foolishness as an excuse to cut and run from uncomfortable truths – truths that cause them cognitive dissonance because they smash through their self-serving weak justifications for selling out – then Malang may have to work up the discipline to keep his anger in check when having those kinds of discussion. Or more accurately, when trading with that particular figure when having those discussions.

"He's right, you know. That Cult of Victimology mess is a far greater cause of our plight than racism ever was. Especially today."

Another flash of anger bubbled up, triggering a mild headache behind Malang's eyes. They're trying me today, Lord! he thought, with at least quasi-amusement. This character was dark-skinned, overweight like he used to be athletic in his youth but then let himself go never to recover—Malang could tell by his shoulders and arms that there was quality muscle under his rounded frame. Bald with a thin goatee, he dressed in a short-sleeved utility shirt, jeans and workboots, like he just got off a shift at one of the local factor plants. A red ball cap sat on his head turned backwards.

"How much of that discussion did you hear?" asked Malang.

"All of it. I heard both sides if that's what you're asking."

"Okay, that's interesting. Do you mind explaining how this 'victimology' concept functions exactly? Just so I'm clear."

"Well, there is no racism. Not the way it used to be. Bottomline. But people built playing victims to imaginary racism into Black culture and that ain't right at all! It means we just want to stay separate on the outside of American and cry about how unfair everything is instead of integrating into the rest of society. Do we have to take a backseat to them whites? Yeah! They own everything. Is it unfair that the ones who own everything determine how far we can get and shit like that? Maybe. But is it better to sit outside hungry in the dirt crying about how unfair it is, or getting up, making yourself presentable according to the pay master's standards, and get in there and get a job so you and your family will be alright? How does crying victim help us at all? It DON'T!"

"How do you define racism, please?"

"It's treating people inferior based on the color of their skin."

"And you don't think white people—the 'pay masters,' as you called them—are doing that?"

"Nah! They look down on us with contempt because of how we choose to behave! I have contempt on us, TOO!"

"So, let me summarize your position about the Black American so I'm clear. Please correct me if I've gotten it wrong."

"Bet."

"You believe that even though the Black American was put in an artificial impoverished state by 'old racism' through no fault of his own, he is just 'playing victim' when he protests the unfair treatment and limited opportunities offered to him by the very guy who benefited from all of that 'old racism' and instead demands the full economic inclusion he was owed since the end of slavery."

"Owed?" asked the red-capped gentleman. "How are we owed?"

"The 230 yrs of chattel slavery, robbed us of our ability to accrue wealth to pass down as inheritance to our descendants. That's one aspect of our artificial impoverished state. Another is the multi-layered discriminatory practices and violent terror and plunder inflicted upon us in the 150 yrs after slavery, all of which continued to prevent us from amassing wealth of our own, since for 400 yrs now, our would-be inheritance has gone into the hoarded wealth coffers of your pay masters. It's why inheritance wealth performs better than labor does in the markets, because the profits of labor generated by Black Americans has been taken and added to the ill-gotten inheritance of the white racist aristocracy."

"Maaaan…"

"The nature of racism is economic," Malang continued. "It always has been. The economic damage done to us is astronomical and our government – complicit in the wrong done to us at every step of the way – is the one who owes us to make it right. We deserve to be made whole. Not only economically with the closure of the lineage-based racial wealth gap, but we deserve to be protected in a wealth-building ownership class, free from further molestation by the greedy fiend."

"Man, white people ain't gone do all of that! They ain't gone give you shit! You crazy as hell if you think they will!"

"Would it be better to continue the struggle using all the tools at hand, with determination and patient perseverance until we get what we are owed—however long it takes!—or would it be better to do what the whites want and just surrender into their anti-Black racist terms, shufflin', grinnin' and dancin' so we don't offend your precious pay masters?"

"All I know is that Gregory Evans is gone do HIM!" he said, dramatically pounding his chest. "You see what I'm sayin'?! Fuck all that YOU talkin' about!"

"Does the very idea of fighting until we are free disturb you, Gregory? Are you offended at the very idea that we, too, would become pay masters, equal to our white rivals, competing equally with him—eye to eye!—in the open free markets? Do you hate this idea?"

"The shit's IMPOSSIBLE, man!"

"It's not impossible," Malang said patiently. Amused, he noticed it was easier to maintain his own cool when his opponent blew his top. "We can win as long as we are together and never give up, in God's Name."

* * *

Gently bouncing Olivia on her hip, Margaret holds the door open to the garage for Malang as he steps up into the house foyer. They kiss and he kisses Margaret around ger face and growls kissing into her neck, making her giggle. Malang takes the now squirming 18-month-old from her and coos while she grabs his face with tiny plump hands. "How was it, bae?"

"Oh, it was good. A lot of great dialogue with good groups gathering and lingering to listen."

"Did you sell any of them?"

"No." Malang switched Olivia from a cradle hold to putting her up on his shoulder. She immediately grabbed his ear. "There were a few almost buys. One lady said she was interested in anything with a 'black-girl-magic' theme and I said I'd bring some tomorrow."

"Alright."

"Yeah, it's okay. Selling the prints isn't actually the poin-!"

"And what IS the point again?" asked Margaret interrupting him.

"Well, there's two points to it. The first point is to take the One God at His Word by choosing a worthy cause to patiently persevere through with all sincerity and faith. God said He is with those who perform this good deed and if the Lord is with me, how can I lose?"

"Okay, I agree." Margaret leaned back against the stair railing post, seeming to relax some. She wore a black skirt falling just above her medium-brown toned bare feet, with a sleeveless purple blowse.

"The other point is to spread awareness – from my own understanding – of the worthy cause that I have chosen. In general, this is anti-racism scholarship. In specific, this is the pro-Reparations movement, which includes closing the lineage-based racial wealth gap, making the Black American former slave class economically whole. When I started this journey, I was resigned to figuring out how to do it all on my own. I thought I was going to have to dig through the ruins of the Civil Rights Era to cobble back together the Black Economic Empowerment message to rekindle that flame myself, but fortunately I don't have to do all of that. I'm blessed to have found during the course of my studies the American Descendants of Slavery (ADOS) group. Founded by

Las Californias criminal attorney Antonio Moore and former Democratic Party aid Yvette Carnell, it's a legitimate organic, nation-wide grassroots movement – data driven by warrior scholars who are all about speaking truth to power – this is the real thing. They've picked up the baton dropped by the slain Dr. Martin Luther King, Jr., and they are actively empowering the people through knowledge of the political game to come together to pressure their… OUR… U.S. government for the transformational politics long withheld from us for centuries. This is where we all should be and I am honored, blessed to lend my voice, talents and skills to help them help our people, in the Name of God."

"American Descendants of what, you said?"

"American Descendants of Slavery."

"I don't like that," said Margaret with a frown.

"You don't like the name? It perfectly describes our ethnic group, aligned with our unique lineage and heritage."

"Well, I don't like that it has 'slavery' in it."

"Really?" asked Malang. "Why?"

"It's gross. Belittling. It makes me feel bad hearing it."

"Why would that make you feel bad? We aren't the ones who made us slaves, who permanently delegated our ancestors to the bondsmen class. We didn't do anything wrong. On the contrary, we were a believing people, even against the odds, and we persevered, surviving the most brutal type of slavery that was ever created for 230 years."

"That's true."

"Yeah, and along the way, we not only created the wealthiest nation on earth, but from the eclectic scraps of torn apart memory we built a brand new culture from scratch that is the most copied, exploited, sought after and envied in the whole world. The former slave class did these things and we have nothing to be ashamed of at all in acknowledging the truth of our heritage."

Margaret smiled, closed her eyes and shook her head, the natural black curls of her fluffy ponytail bun bouncing gently with the movement. "What?" he asked.

She looked up at him with a gleam in her eyes. "I just love you." The two smiled at each other and the baby squealed.

* * *

The night found Malang in his den, reading through some of his research materials to strengthen his mind for the next day's work. After putting his family to bed, he quietly moved down the hall to enter into this curious new aspect of his life that his private workroom now represented. Almost overwhelming on some days, Malang's deep-dive into anti-racism scholarship ignited a passion that threatened to feel too big for his art skills, still sometimes making him wonder if he was using the correct method of expression. He paused in his readings, a refresher on the nightmarishly evil land theft protocols unleashed upon Black American farmers just inside of the last fifty years, to think about the two points he had described to his wife earlier. The passion making him feel as if his art might not be enough is different from actually feeling the pangs of doubt that this is so. The latter was answered definitely by Malang spontaneously slipping into a trance state to bear witness to the sign of the Wisdom Eye. This most mysterious and misunderstood gift of the spirit assured him he was indeed on the right path and all was well. Suddenly feeling very moved, he sat up and recited a prayer of thanks to his Guardian Lord who made Malang and all of humankind. He thanked God for His blessings & favor, for His fatefulness, mercy and for being TRUE.

"…and count me among those who are grateful. Amen."

Suddenly excited—he could feel his eyes widening like saucers in anticipation—Malang felt the unmistakable tingling body infusion of The Serpent Fire of the Universe wash over him. Is it going to happen again? he thought, recalling that the Serpent Fire feeling exactly this intense heralded both 'third eye' opening events. Despite waiting a good ten minutes poised for another wonderful, altered state of consciousness journey, the energy dissipated without it. Malang felt neither disappointment nor longing (who is he to express vulgar and uncouth entitlement over a spirit gift?), and simply went back to his reading.

When he reached a natural stopping point, he opened a popular video streaming application to recharge his batteries by listening to Antonio & Yvette, the two #ADOS movement founders, as they broke down the data and carefully instructed their dutiful subscribers, such as Malang, what the next move should be for the American Descendants of Slavery to achieve the transformational politics required to ascend beyond the artificially improved culture of struggle-survival into the thriving protected class that is their birthright. Malang quietly prepared a cup of lemon honey tea, his choice of libation as a mock obligatory requirement for watching Yvette's BreakingBrown channel offerings. He smiled at the playful running gag of Yvette and her subscribers.

Yvette announced the formal launch of the "ADOS Advocacy Foundation (ADOSAF)," explaining that everything had already been done as far as a loose, nonorganized group could take the movement – it was now time to level up for the goal of effective collective uplift of the Black American identity group. Malang listened with interest, taking careful notes.

"Power is always organized," said Yvette, repeating herself for effect. "This is a move towards a disciplined movement with a transformative Black Agenda and Reparations as the cornerstone. That's why this had to happen this way." Malang followed the channel links to the official ADOSAF website (adosfoundation.org), absorbing the Mission Statement, repeating key parts aloud that moved him:

"Ours is an experience defined by the unique, shared cost of multigenerational plunder. And as we stand in the shoes of our ancestors, we insist upon a specific group designation as essential to this undertaking. […] A debt must be paid, and our inheritance protected. We insist upon an historic, targeted allotment of policy and protections that fulfills the promise of economic inclusion and integrates the descendants of chattel slavery into the drivers of wealth."

* * *

While driving up to the jazz festival the next morning, Malang found himself sitting at what had to be the longest red light in all of Chocolate City. Or maybe even all of the East Coast, he thought wryly. He decided he could probably use such moments to practice building the discipline of patience—being conscious of his feelings and recognizing that all such moments are little tests—since his new 'patient perseverance' mantra was the driving force of his art activism life nowadays. Of course, it would be ridiculous to assume that sitting patiently at a red light could possibly be considered a formal good deed on the Lord's Judgment score card, yet using these opportunities to strengthen his character in that regard would obviously strengthen his spiritual toolkit by extension. He breathed in deeply through his nose and mouth at the same time, then exhaled with enough force to make the sound, "sah." He meditated on what Yvette Carnell said in her clip last night, specifically about the need to protect the ADOS movement from any Tom, Dick and Tariq who would want to say just whatever about the movement while making dubious claims of their own affiliation. Malang Flathill was not a formal member of the official organization himself. Not yet. He readily admitted to himself that he enjoyed the independence and autonomy that came with the pre-incorporation into an organized entity, with the freedom to express his full support from his own interpretation of the founders' materials, but the last thing he'd want to do is overstep his bounds and offend them or the rest of the inner circle members. Malang felt that this organization was the real deal and that supporting it was the key to not only his people finally being made whole in this country they built, but it was also the key to his own personal salvation as a believer in the Most-High. Would he be able to move forward in promoting pro-ADOS art in his own way to both remain independent in a win/win…? Malang was not quite sure, but he was determined to…

HONK HONNNK!!!

Malang jerked forward in his burgundy Japanese model sedan and drove on through the green light, his face tingling from the embarrassed flush of Adrenalin. Amused with himself, he directed a scientific comparative analysis probe towards noticing just how different that embarrassed tingle felt compared to that of The Serpent Fire of the Universe.

* * *

"I like it," said Patricia, her over-bedazzled jeweled glasses dancing in the early morning sunlight. "How much?" Malang quoted her a price for the first 18"x24" #BlackGirlMagic print he showed her, the rest displayed on easels just behind. She nodded and stepped around to study the other two. The themed messaging showed the popular concept used as a diabolical tactic of 'divide & conquer' designed to split up the ADOS family by elevating the Black American woman to loyal support class attendant in white-owned spaces, while her ADOS counterpart was torn down and prepared for convict leasing abuses within the anti-ADOS mass incarcerate 'gray wastes.' To Malang's surprise, Patricia bought all four, with him carefully and self-consciously wrapping them securely and then carrying them to her white Silverado. He watched her impressively climb and swing her 4 ft nothing frame up and into the cab. They exchanged mutually courteous pleasantries and he returned to his booth. His Dashiki neighbor awaited him, staring at the same print that seemed to irritate him the other day.

Dashiki guy barely let a grunt escape him when they greeted each other during the morning setup. He acted like he didn't want to hold the gate open for Malang either, though he didn't change his own tempered etiquette in return. Malang predicted his sensitive neighbor was going to need some time to process his feelings about the piece before he was ready to vent about it. Apparently now was the time.

"I just want to know whether you intended this to be serious?"

"I'm sorry, what's your name?"

"Kenneth."

"Good morning, Kenneth," said Malang laughing. "I guess this one really spoke to you, huh?"

"At first I thought it meant you were one of those Black Republican guys who've been mouthing off lately about 'shithole' countries and what not, but then I heard you arguing with those two from yesterday, so it can't be that. I don't think so anyway. Basically, I guess I'm asking what's your angle? Is it just for shock value?"

"It's not a shock value piece, no. The message is very serious, and the piece is designed to get the Black ethnic groups talking about what it means, to ignite a dialogue that can possibly lead to understanding and fixing the issue that the print caricatures."

"So, you think this is real?"

"It is real."

"No, it's not!" said Kenneth firmly. "Look, this is exactly the type of mess the white man wants. How do you not see that? Black people attacking Black people. I think this is really irresponsible and definitely offensive to display at the Chocolate City jazz fest. Are you serious? It's crazy!"

"Judging by your reaction," said Malang. "It sounds like you're saying that the message of the piece isn't true. If this is accurate, what are you basing this opinion on?"

"Why are you trying to separate Black people?! Are you an agent of white supremacy? Division is the last thing we need!"

"My problem with that point of view is that, as the American Descendants of Slavery, no one in the last 50-60 years at least believed in the "Pan-African" unified Black people concept more than us. My entire Black Generation-X demographic was thoroughly indoctrinated in it. So, imagine my shock and hurt when, after my group became conscious of the need to unify along our unique lineage & heritage to use our organized power to fight for the transformational politics we desperately need, the other Black ethnic groups here as immigrants and the children of immigrants…"

"We're ALL immigrants here, man," Kenneth interrupted."

"No," snapped Malang with obvious annoyance. "The immigrant comes here on purpose looking for a better life. My people were brought here against their will in those great stinking hips. I am no damned immigrant." Malang watched Kenneth's face work in mild confusion for a brief moment. When no response seemed forth-coming he continued his point. "Even though my government has deliberately withheld for centuries the inheritance debt that it owes me with a robust Reparatory Justice program and economic inclusion in a protected, wealth-building owner class, the very idea of me leveraging my dormant political might to retrieve it was not supported by the Black immigrants. They immediately got on camera to assure white people that 'we' didn't need Reparations. Can you see that this behavior meant that the "unified Black diaspora" wasn't doing anything for me in all these decades since The Immigration and Nationality Act of 1965 was passed? I'm politically disenfranchised today because the Black immigrant figure was brought here to counter the 1964 Civil Rights and 1965 Voting Rights Acts. The white racist aristocracy proved more than willing to pretend the Black immigrant was the 'new face of Black America' since they didn't have my baggage and could be convinced not to compete fairly in the markets against whites. I deserve to compete fairly in the markets as an economic equal, but also as the protected class elite who made the USA's great opportunities possible!"

"All of that is your case huh? You're just a conspiracy theorist!"

"Is that really your response?"

Kenneth bristled. "You didn't say anything to respond to! The bottom-line is that Black people need to come together to fight racism! Period!"

"Well, we do need to come together, but there's a way that needs to be done. Of all of the Black diaspora, the Black American ethnic group is the only one who is disenfranchised from his own country, locked out of access to capital and credit and told not to do what all other political identity groups have done to succeed. We, too, need to first become strong as a self-interested, political identity group and only THEN can we interconnect with other like Black special interest groups for mutual win/wins. History has shown – recent history, mind you – that if we are scattered and disunified, joining with our skinfolk brethren will only lead to our exploitation and plunder. Et tu, 'brother?'"

"What's crazy is you keep talking like Black Americans are the only ones who have ever experienced racism!"

"That's a strawman fallacy. That's not my argument. I agree that Black people from around the world deal with similar problems born from the savagery of European Imperialist blight across the globe. Of course. But my group has a very specific history with our white dominated government and they owe us a very specific debt based on what they specifically did to US. Just like the other Black ethnic groups had very specific histories with the European nations that conquered the regions their people lived in. You can't leave that problem, come to MY home and tell my enemy that 'WE' don't need my debt paid for the accrued discrimination done to ME!"

"All I'm saying is that it's impossible to fight white people if we aren't together! Divisiveness is the last thing we need!"

"Hey, telling the long-suffering people in the land you deliberately moved to that they don't need their Reparations because you are rich and don't need it is definitely 'divisiveness' in the exact way evil white racists would want to see divisiveness among us, Kenneth. It's certainly not a demonstration of any type of unity I would ever want to be a part of."

"Man, you just like to hear yourself talk!"

"I like to actually finish my point before my opponent responds. I prefer a well-ordered debate in which we take turns expressing ourselves civilly. Please go ahead and make your point." A small group had gathered to listen by this point. Although seemingly engaged, many expressed a hostile disapproval of Malang's position. Not surprising since there were quite a few Black immigrant entrepreneurs present, all attracted by the big jazz festival crowds. Malang didn't necessarily want to alienate his people's skinfolk by laying the facts bare, but what good would hiding from the truth leave behind? His people were the wealthless bottom caste of this country they built and no one can say they got there because they DIDN'T grow up being taught Pan-Africanism's "flat blackness" ideals as virtue.

"What I want to know is can we at least agree that we need to come together like white people do?"

"Why would I agree to that?" asked Malang.

"WHAT?"

"White people invented the idea of forming an economic-based group identity around racial phenotype. It only worked at all because it was driven by a few dozen ruthless legacy families who slaughtered all of their Euro-ethnic potential competition throughout the Old World basically during the rise of the red communist state in the 20th century. Coming together over the loving gaze of mammon's amassed hoards of stolen loot was successful for them when you're willing to torture and kill literally everybody. How are you realistically suggesting the Black diaspora come together in the same way without an equally sociopathic focused vision based on the devil's blueprint of kill, steal and destroy?"

"You don't think we need to come together as Black people to stop white supremacy?" asked

Kenneth incredulously.

"No. There is nothing at all inherently good about the idea of unifying along racial phenotype lines. It's never been done before now, and whites only invented the idea based on barbaric greed. It's not even working for them, really."

"You could have fooled me! Look at them!"

"I think in the end, all that 'whiteness' did was allow the usual suspects – the 1% grifting legacy families who have always schemed to rule over humans in one form or another even way before the rise of the European Imperialist Age – to create a false narrative to hide behind to do what they have always done… hoard the majority of wealth & resources just for themselves and pretend to be living idols or whatever. Most of the world's wealth is in the hands of the modern 1% class, with some trickle down to lesser economic classes among the white racist aristocracy to keep them loyal to the team. As long as the Black American is around for them to target and release their entitled brat rages upon, the majority of whites are easy for the 1% to control. We are useful to them as a 'flat blackness' tool of mass social engineering, so why would I assume that their own unnatural invention designed specifically to exploit me is magically holy the way the Pan-Africans believe? It's ridiculous. The Pan-African reminds me of the Satanists, in how their entire shtick is to deliberately flip Christian symbolism around backwards to make a rebel without a cause statement of shallow defiance. Flipping white supremacy around in a funhouse mirror to impotently prop up a 'black supremacy' has the same level of goofy mock seriousness to it."

"You insult the ancestors," said Kenneth gravely, shaking his head.

"I forgive them for their folly, for they did not know."

"YOU forgive THEM???"

"It's easy to see how a people who knew only assault and molestation at the hands of 'whiteness' could be convinced by a succession of smooth-talking slicksters, eager in their lust to woo the loyalty of this same group whose blood, sweat & tears built the wealthiest nation in recorded history, that 'blackness' was the only thing that could defeat their foe."

"What 'smooth-talking slicksters?'"

"Marcus Garvey, Noble Drew Ali, Wallace Fard, Elijah Mohammed… the who's who of 'spiritual grifters' who showed up proclaiming themselves to be prophets of God, et cetera, who thought that if they moved fast enough they could build an army cult of Black Americans to compete successfully against whites and make their fortunes as modern pharaohs at our expense."

"I have never heard anyone talk this crazy... a Black man! Bro, I hate to say this, but you're a coon. For real. You're insulting our ancestors! Our great leaders!"

"You think I'm a 'coon' for calling these characters out based on the fruit of what they did and how the lives of Black Americans didn't improve once these folk showed up. To a man they all just set themselves up as cult leader figures and lived like mini-lords and demanded loyalty from the throngs they convinced to serve them. For what? How has that helped us?"

"Man, you need to help yourself, bruh."

"Yeah?" responded Malang with a grin. "So, they didn't show up to help us at all?"

"If you have the wrong attitude and don't accept their teachings – recognize them as great men! – then they can't help you. Show them the proper respect and they..."

"Will give me a position in their cult organization that is all about them and not the group uplift we need to be made whole. No thanks."

"Well, what are you doing now?!" Kenneth shouted.

"Am I hearing right?" asked Malang. "Did you just ask, in an emotional outburst, what am I doing now in my life that's so important that I'm not willing to be a cult leader's stooge?"

"You're twisting my words! That's not even what I said!"

"I'm not twisting your words, I'm asking your question back to you in my own words. If that isn't what you are saying then tell me what you really meant then. Remember, I'm currently free and at liberty to live my life how I like, as opposed to giving away my freedoms to willingly submit myself to the fickle whims of these mere humans who want me to think they are living idols to be quasi-worshiped. Nothing at all about that is attractive to me. What am I doing now, you ask? Whatever I like, without having to get the permission of Sheikh Aboo-boo first."

"Maybe if you weren't so arrogant…"

"You don't think these jokers are/were arrogant?" asked Malang. "Really?"

"I'm saying that just maybe if you had the ear to hear truth that was beyond your understanding, you'd…"

"Want to be the subjugated stooge to some trumped up guy?"

"…change your mind about them and wouldn't be so quick to disrespect them."

"Am I disrespecting them by pointing out these fake religious cult leader grifters didn't provide my ethnic group any value? My actual Black Leaders from the time period did provide value—you know them by the fruit they bear—and conspicuously they were shot by our enemies. Note that none of the charismatic, self-serving cult leader grifters got shot?"

"Al-Hajj Malik Al-Shabazz!"

"What about him?"

"Wasn't he a 'cult leader' as you call it in Elijah's organization?"

"I remember he was put out of the organization for butting heads with the actual cult leader, formed his own organization that was conspicuously absent the pseudo-spiritual gobbledygook of his former mentor, wrote a serious Black Political Agenda, and was then killed. Malcolm was the real deal, not a fraud like the rest of them."

"Are you gone disrespect him in the same breath as you praise him by calling him by his slave name though?"

"Are you going to derail the discussion by harping on a triviality? I'm not insisting on calling him by the other name out of spite, I just call him that interchangeably because he was very famous and known more by that name. His autobiography is titled by that name and where my generation learned about him, right? Calm down. I love that brother and consider him a personal influence as do many of us."

"Bruh, I think we're just gonna have to agree to

disagree," said Kenneth, with a melodramatic hand wave.

"Yeah?" said Malang. "And to be clear, what are we agreeing to disagree about exactly? You agree that Black immigrants should be allowed to erase/replace the Black American on behalf of the desires of white people since they don't have our American historical baggage, versus me 100% disagreeing with that?"

"That's not what I believe!"

"That's what Pan-Africanism's 'flat blackness' represents."

Kenneth briskly walked back over to his booth, grumbling under his breath. Malang watched him with a sad amusement. No wonder the guy took so long to finally voice his opinion… he had nothing to counter the print's message with other than the butthurt of cognitive dissonance flare ups, Malang thought. Apparently, he expected to win whatever his argument was supposed to be with the force of his emotion and appeals to Malang's abstract sense of magical melanin alone. He turned towards the river of slowly moving jazz festival patrons and continued to engage until the end of the day, encouraging the Black Americans who showed interest in his work to check out the #ADOS movement.

3

Bring On the Trolls

The next weekend after the Chocolate City Jazz Festival found Malang Flathill holding down a booth in the Cyprus Trade Center, one of two large indoor flea market facilities found in the midst of the suburban townships surrounding the Chocolate City area.

After the booming enthusiasm of the jazz festival crowd, the sparser patron movement at Cyprus seemed almost sad, but Malang found himself more engaged in discussion by 10am Saturday than he had been by the same time last weekend. A light sheen of sweat formed on his brow, revealing the main difference between the two venues was in the level of intensity brought by the attention his anti-racism messaging attracted. Even though much of the jazz festival attention he received were argumentative opposing viewpoints, they were still from his own ethnic group and race and there was a line that wasn't crossed no matter how heated the topics got.

This was not the case at the Cyprus Trade Center.

"HORSESHIT!!! Reparations or nothing else is owed to you people! First of all, there was only a tiny percentage of whites who even owned slaves, and an even tinier percentage of modern whites descended from slave owners!" This from the owner of the business directly across the aisle, his proud display of deer hunter merchandise taking up two booths. In a sleeveless grey t-shirt, knee-length jean shorts and dirty pink foam clogs, his red ball cap almost fell off the top of his flushed pink, sweaty bald head from all of his animated jerking about.

"The number of actual slave owners doesn't effect whether my people get their over-due Reparations or not, Bill," said Malang. "What matters is that my people were enslaved, they did provide free slave labor in a national economy that was 100% dependent upon it to create unprecedented super-wealth that everyone benefited from except my people. Remember that as a slave, the fruit of their labor was taken by someone else, preventing them from accruing their own wealth to pass down to their descendants, hence why my people didn't have anything at all come the formal abolishment of the chattel institution. It was the government's job to fix it, to make us economically whole after being complicit in our systemic exploitation."

Bill couldn't wait to interrupt. "All the lives lost—on BOTH sides!—during the war, not to mention the estimated billions in today's dollars of destruction caused, should be considered 'reparations' enough, since the whole point of the thing was to emancipate the slaves!"

"Is THAT what you lot go around telling yourselves now? That's weird. The reality of the matter is that the Southern planters wanted to expand their Über-lucrative enterprise further south into Central and South America, to give all able-bodied white men the opportunity to become faux-lords with plantations of Black slaves and King Cotton wealth. The president told them, 'No,' and they defiantly decided to secede and do it anyway which triggered the Civil War... the actual point of which was to punish the Confederates for their insolence and keep the Union together. Freeing the slaves was only ever a desperate war tactic designed to snatch the rug out from under the traitors, it was never a goal of the war itself."

"Well, regardless...!"

"'Regardless,' WHAT? White men playing war games based on greed. That's the nature of that entire event. At the end of it, my people found ourselves freed from an evil system that we were tossed into through zero fault of our own. As American citizens, we rightfully deserved to have our government do right by us and use its spending power to make up for the previous 230 yrs of evils it allowed to be inflicted upon us and it benefited from."

"YOUR PEOPLE?! Ha! That's the kind of divisive talk that has caused all of these problems in the first place!" shouted Bill.

"So, the problems started, not with the selfish and evil decision to permanently delegate the enslaved Black African to a bondsman class, but at the point where their descendants protest the legacy of continued poor treatments and demanded Reparatory Justice?"

"You're puttin' words in my mouth!"

Malang chuckled. "Okay, then please elaborate on this idea that modern 'divisive talk' is what 'caused all the problems.' Just so we're both clear what you are actually talking about."

"It's simple! Everything was fine… NOW HEAR ME OUT!" shouted Bill as Malang visibly bristled at the word 'fine.' "Hear me out!"

"No, go ahead. I'm all ears." Malang leaned a hand on his blueish-grey folding chair and flashed a sardonic grin.

"These libtard communist pricks are the ones who started stirring up the trouble! They're the ones who fanned the flames of old resentment which ignited into the Civil Rights thing! So, now you have all of these 'social justice warriors' creating a climate of entitled fake hubris as an overreaction to what happened in the 1960s! Instead of just letting it go and moving forward, you activist types want to force innocent white people to pay 'reparations' checks for something that happened 152 years ago and just deepen racial resentments and create additional problems."

"Alright, so let me summarize what it sounds like you are saying to me."

"Go 'head," said Bill, folding his massive, hairy arms across his chest.

"You're telling me that even though Black people were prevented from accruing generational wealth during the 230 yrs of slavery and had nothing when slavery was abolished, were terrorized and lynched for the next 100 yrs to prevent them from becoming competitive, economic equals with whites in the markets and had their land stolen, were systemically criminalized to return them to slavery under the convict leasing programs, were returned to second class citizenship under forced jim crow segregation that everything was 'fine' and it was only their efforts to finally truly be free during the turbulent civil rights era that any problems started. Those problems being that Black people wouldn't shut up and just be 'fine.'"

"See, you're just letting those libtards fill your head with…"

"So, I'm not able to research/read history for myself then? Someone else had to spoonfeed I to me in an act of brainwashing, huh?"

"LOOK! IF YOU WANT TO GO AROUND BEING A DAMNED VICTIM ALL THE TIME THEN GO AHEAD!!!" shouted Bill from behind a beet-red face.

Malang gave out a hearty laugh. "I'm just trying to understand your position!" he said, raising his hands and shoulders in an innocence posture. "It sounds like you want me to ignore documented history to instead believe… what? What you are telling me right now?"

"Well…"

"Okay, then at least tell me where you are getting YOUR information about the historic record from? Since you think all books are written by your partisan rivals…"

"Not all!! I didn't say all!"

"Some books you do like." Another chuckle from Malang. "Fine. That's a breakthrough, I think. May I assume that all the books you like were written by people who think exactly like you do, which as far as you've revealed here this morning, would be the functional equivalent to reading the Confederacy's constitution for their planned secession." Malang laughed again and Bill's face worked as if he was both stuck from a lack of words and ready to explode again. "Tell me why I should accept your version of history as true. How will this benefit me? In what way? Go."

"You'll have peace of mind, some money in your pocket, and some pride in yourself by not carrying around this victim attitude the libtards got you on."

"You don't think I was a literal victim during all that Ku Klux Klan lynching business…?"

"No! They only lynched criminals!"

"How convenient."

"There's no proof that the Klan were…"

"Were lynching people? Bill, they ran those killing in the newspapers. Newspaper articles aren't proof now? I'm pretty sure they are. Okay, you said that if I decide to take what you're going on about at face value, it means I'll 'have some money in my pocket.' That's weird, since we both know you not only don't agree with me receiving my long overdue Reparations, you also don't believe in Black Americans being competitive wealth-building equals with white people in the open free markets. So, where is this 'money in my pocket' supposed to come from if I hang out with you?"

"Jobs!" Bill shouted triumphantly. "Pay from an honest day's work."

"So, if I'm not in the wealth-building ownership class as a competitive economic equal with white people, that means I'm just an employee in a white-owned business. If I do have my own business, I have to take the leftover scraps after whites in colluding partnership with their cronies in local government get all the big lucrative contracts I'm locked out of. If I hang out with you, I can only ever aspire to being a servant-like support class helping you get richer while I watch. And you think that situation is just 'fine.'"

"What I don't like is you like to twist everything into you being a victim!"

"I don't have to do much twisting certainly. You know that the advocacy for transformational politics will make me whole and finally a full American citizen, right? That's the only way to cure my 'victimhood' you're always complaining about, but you are continuously against me working the political system in order to get what I need so we can stop being victimized…"

"YOU AREN'T BEING VICTIMIZED!!! That's just the libtards talking through you!"

"No, I'm definitely being exploited & plundered and prevented from being an American. You want me to ignore the facts of history and believe the yarn you guy's spin. If I do that, I'll be a spineless coward betraying my ethnic group, yes?"

Bill shook his head vigorously. "I disagree."

"You disagree with what?"

"The way you stop being a damned victim is by changing your damned attitude!"

"You want me to just relax into being abused…"

"YOU'RE NOT BEING ABUSED!!!!"

"You want me to pretend that I'm not being abused and just relax into the abuse and accept it. The difference between being a victim or not is confronting the truth of being victimized by the greediest savages on earth versus walking around in a La-La Land fantasy as if nothing is wrong so that the one victimizing can enjoy the spoils of his ill-gotten hoards without hearing complaints."

"You're just committed to being a victim, huh?"

"No! I'm committed to the political advocacy I need to perform so I can engineer the victimization of my people out of our communities. You want me to just turn the other cheek or whatever and be alright with being victimized."

"What's this Reparations going to fix anyway?" asked Bill.

"My artificial impoverishment. Is that a real question?"

"It's not gonna fix shit! All it will do is make you want more and more and it will never end!"

"It sounds like you think that my reparations program would just be a one-time check. That's ridiculously naïve considering it took generations to put me in a wealthless bottom caste state, right? I've spent most of my time in my country being subjugated into artificial impoverishment to make it easier for others to exploit me. Naturally it will take several generations of focused government payments and programs to pull me out of poverty, both physically and mentally. It'll take at LEAST the multi-generational effort it took to pull the poor whites and immigrants out of poverty in the late 19th and early 20th centuries with all the free land grants and New Deal gibs and stuff, right? So, if you all received all of that to make sure you were alright, how could I receive anything less? Closing the racial wealth gap needs to be an 'as long as it takes' effort."

"And who's going to pay for all of that?!"

"Why ask me that? Who paid for whites to receive the trillions and trillions of dollars of gibs and land you all received? Are you asking me a question that does little more than you reveal you think your group is magically more worthy of the good life than my group? Then you have the nerve to protest when people mention 'white entitlement.'"

Malang refused to give an inch during the heated exchange, with Bill growing only increasingly frustrated mainly due to discovering that concepts that he matter-of-factly assumed were "just common sense!" crumbled before his eyes with a minimum of pushback…

…from a Black American man.

Since his clan had brainwashed themselves into thinking that Black Americans were inherently of inferior intelligence to whites, this encounter caused him no end of cognitive dissonance, primarily manifesting in his beet-red sweaty face and aggravated ulcer. Bill kept to his own booth for the rest of that day, Malang catching his eye occasionally to see a clear pout. At the end of the work day, Malang engaged a friendly early middle-aged Black American couple, their interest in the ADOS Advocacy Foundation causing his voice to rise a bit with the force of excited passion. Malang was vaguely aware of Bill standing closer to hear him better, but he dismissed it out of hand.

"One of the co-founders, Yvette Carnell, said that the organization would have grown faster if talented Black Americans were less concerned with lifting #ADOS talking points to compete with rival groups, but everyone has that individualist mentality of the toxic 'Integration' age. She's right and I think that more of us will get on board as the momentum of political wins increases and it stands out as the real thing surrounded by a sea of grifters and wannabes. The fact that the #ADOS activists were about to defeat the Harvard Kennedy School when they supported a hostile group of liberal, skinfolk immigrants and sellouts in their efforts to smear the movement and damage the founders' reputations. A relentless pressure of speaking truth to that power would topple that goliath, forcing them in shame to retract the paper. It was beautiful watching them win, and proof positive that #ADOSAF is the way forward for our people, the American Descendants of Slavery."

"It sounds amazing! What could we do to support them?" asked Jamila, looking down at the ADOS Advocacy Foundation leaflet that Malang had printed out. She held it with one hand while the other arm wrapped around her husband's waist.

"The organization and the movement are still in their child-stage and need volunteers, bodies and funds. If the largest, most powerful non-profit orgs are continuously courting big money with fundraisers, it should go without saying that the worthiest cause of all that is only just getting its legs under it could use all of that, too."

"You right!" Pierce and Jamila said in near unison, laughing with Malang. Bill, still hovering in the near background, made a sneering pantomimed gesture to mock the moment.

"Actually, what they could use is talented, skilled and dedicated members who can do the deep political work... the phone calls, the writing... develop legislative strategy to organize our people to take on our government."

Bill wandered back over to his booth as the three continued to talk. The next day, a second man had joined the deer hunter merchandise booth. Looking to be in his early 1960s with close-cropped white hair, the new guy was overweight, standing roughly at Malang's height. He wore a dark blue, button-down dress shirt that was so big it functioned more like a muumuu. We sauntered over and gave a critical assessment of Malang's artwork prints and #ADOS materials with one hand in the pocket of his black jeans, the other holding a popular name brand coffee. Liberal lover, thought Malang with a mocking sniff.

"Good morning," said Malang. "Another hunter, hm? Are you and Bill related?"

The guy cut his eyes at Malang. "He's my nephew. Look, why are you here?"

"What do you mean?"

"Are you supposed to be causing trouble or something?"

"What kind of trouble?"

"Don't know. You tell me." Just like that, the new guy's face flushed just as red as Bill's did yesterday. Yeah, they're related alright, an amused Malang thought.

"I'm here to engage the crowd over topics important to me and my identity group—awareness of certain concepts needs to be spread wide so that people can have Candid & Courageous Conversations over them that can help motivate the people to action."

"I don't know what all of that mumbo-jumbo means."

"In short, I'm advocating for transformational politics to economically include my Black American ethnic group and close the lineage-based racial wealth gap. I certainly hope you don't consider that very worthy cause to be 'causing trouble.'" Malang grinned.

"I think you'd be better off in your own urban community preaching solutions that need your own people to implement."

"That's literally what I'm doing. The transformational politics we need requires us to do the work of politics."

"'Politics' is not going to stop all that black-on-black crime! Acting like a goddamned civilized human being will! Start there!"

"Whoa. Why are you being so heated about it? I don't even know your name and…"

"Fred!"

"…already you are getting all hot & bothered. You don't think that's strange?"

"I think it's strange that you are ignoring your own people's problems while pushing some damned race hustlin' fantasy!"

"Well, I think it's weird that you are so angrily passionate about this topic when you don't speak on the root cause of the problems in our community. You act like the whole thing was our fault alone."

"Slavery was centuries ago and you want to act like it has some bearing on modern problems?! Horseshit!"

"Slavery ended nearly exactly 150 years ago to the day, that 150-year timeframe full of white racist group domestic terror, legal forced jim row segregation, predatory corporate exploitation in partnership with corrupt government officials…"

Fred jerked his head back and sounded the perfect imitation of a cartoon "guffaw." All you Black people can do is regurgitate the same ole white liberal fed myths of victimization. Pathetic."

"Myths? So, if we have no basis of truth to stand upon in a civil discussion, there's no point in continuing. To you be your way and to me be mine," said Malang, eyes fixed hard as he held Fred's gaze. Fred stared back for a couple of beats then broke eye contact with a slow headshake and a smirk.

"Typical. You can't deal with the hard truths, so you run from the real argument!"

"You don't have an argument, Fred. You reject the historical record as 'myths,' preferring instead to shout your shallow partisan rhetoric at me, that you seem to expect me to swallow just because you said it. No, thanks. I have no use for it." Fred walked back over to Bill's booth where the two engaged in a low-toned, apparently intense discussion. Malang noticed that Bill's shiny, sweaty head was just as red as it was yesterday. It seemed like he wasn't as confident in Fred's performance as the latter's bravado expressed.

Malang straightened up the paperwork on his next and looked up to see a man looking at his prints with his hands behind his back. Nearly overcome with an intense sensation of déjà vu, Malang blinked several times trying to orient himself to recall where he may have seen…

"I remember you. You were at the jazz festival the other day, right?"

The tall, thin-framed male slowly took his hands out from behind his back, the motion looked awkward and alien enough to conjure the image of a spider's legs uncoiling and extending. He stepped forward briskly, his right hand extended. The man didn't seem particularly old, but his pale, blue-veined hand sported several patches of liver spots, his eyes dark and sunken back into his skull. Malang offered his name as he firmly gripped the offered hand. "I know who you are. I've read your blog. I'm Joel."

Malang was surprised to feel his face flushed. His eyes darted over towards Bill and he absurdly imagined briefly that his own medium-brown skin was also flashing a beet red. There was no reason for him to feel bashful that this stranger read his two 'third eye' opening event descriptions, was there? That's why he posted them so people would read them.

"Interesting take," said Joel. "I had a couple of things I wanted to ask you, if you don't mind."

"I don't mind. I'm actually putting myself out here for the discussions. To engage. I'll admit this will be my first time talking about THAT stuff publicly, though." Malang laughed awkwardly and Joel responded with a slight smirk, his eyes looking passed him at his prints.

"After having such a profound spiritual experience—never mind whether it was real, or that it was what you believe it was or not—let's say it was. How do you reconcile that experience with your racist hate art? Don't you think that's going backwards after what you saw?" Malang's eyes darted over to the two deer hunter's again and he felt his face flush, this time all the way around to the back of his neck. The bashfulness produced from a stranger bluntly telling him he had read what amounted to personal diary entries was replaced by a disappointment and annoyance.

"You think my prints are racist hatred? In what way?"

"Oh, come on," said Joel. "Your whole shtick is to make racist stereotyped caricatures of everybody who disagrees with you."

"Wait, what 'racist stereotypes' am I using in

this?" Malang pointed to a print at random. Joel's mouth pursed as he hesitated, his eyes dancing as he searched his mind for what he presumed would be readily assessable. The print featured an overweight drunken white male having urinated on himself as he berated a Black American activist figure.

"Well, maybe it's not a stereotype per se, but you have to admit it is clearly unflattering."

"Am I somehow magically obligated to only flatter white people in my art? What new rule is that?"

"Alright. You're right. Maybe I was overreacting on that one. But could you answer my other question then?"

"I don't think it's 'going backwards' to advocate for my people's economic inclusion and finally becoming free in this land they built. No. Why would it be?"

"It seems like an enlightened being wouldn't care about earthly troubles. Don't you think so?"

"I've never claimed to be 'enlightened,' not in the sense that the far eastern mysticism concepts define the term. I do think the 'third eye' opening is a sign for those on that Path though. I think it's an odd question from my perspective as an Abrahamic theist though. The prophets of the One God were certainly enlightened and nothing in scripture says they cut off their duties to the poor, the widow and the orphan and all those who were less fortunate. They were not only the most charitable in that regard to spend out of God's bounty provided to them to help the needy, but also to fight with might and main in the cause of their Lord against those who would oppress others. How could anyone possibly become enlightened without being in that committed headspace first? I'm of deep disquieting suspicion of any figure who would claim that ascended state without their record of deeds reflecting such truths."

"I see where you're coming from and I can respect it. Personally, I think the Abrahamic religions are problematic, and even you just using words like 'fight' and 'might' in that context are lightyears away from any kind of enlightenment."

"That's interesting," said Malang thoughtfully. "I can't imagine disagreeing with anyone more." His eyes once again darted across the aisle, perhaps coincidently.

Joel laughed. "Well, it's not that serious... not enough to snuff out a potentially good conversation before it even gets going. So, in your opinion, spiritual ascendency goes hand-in-hand with social justice."

"I would go so far as to say that spiritual ascendancy for the human being of planet earth would be impossible without believing in the One God who made us and dedicating ourselves to social justice aligned towards the criteria the One God revealed for that purpose. I'm curious as to how we could become ascended into the high spirit without our material flesh being submitted to righteous."

"That depends on how we define righteousness, right?"

Malang straightened up to his full height. "Righteousness for the human being is submitting oneself to the One God who made him, doing good deeds per God's definition, rejecting evil deeds per God's definition of the term and repenting when we mess up."

Joel flashed yellowed teeth, crooked in towards the center of his slightly sardonic smile. "I don't define righteous in quite so dogmatic terms. I think it's just being open to new experiences to the point of purity. The ultimate 'just do it' and 'go with the flow.' It's less about having some old book tell you how to do it and more like you just know what it is when it happens. The opposite of that is what we'd call evil, which is something that is too rigid and you have to force it."

"Hm," Malang carefully searched Joel's face. "It sounds almost like you're hinting that organized religion is 'evil' in its strict guidance."

"I would have to question your definition of 'evil'

since my own, again, isn't so rigid."

"Joel, did you come here to talk me out of my 'third eye' experience, or to perhaps seek to influence me in what I should think it meant?"

"Not at all!" Joel said laughing. "My main purpose was to see if you still had that copy of Dr. Hessians' book and if you'd be willing to sell it to me."

"Ah. Well, this last minute or two gives me the impression that you also came to probe and see what I was like in other ways as well. I have no interest in paganism in any of its forms, Joel, especially anything that sounds suspiciously like white people trying to fabricate a fake spiritual concept designed to make them feel guilt-free over their commitment to anti-ADOS systemic racism. I am a committed believer in the One God, Supreme Creator of reality and Master of the Day of Judgment. I have zero desire to ignite the Divine's Wrath by rejecting God and running after things that I know He hates above all else."

"Fair enough," said Joel, with a disappointed, subdued low tone. "Although I don't see what race has to do with all of this." His eyes darted away. "And the book then?"

Now it was Malang's turn to laugh. "Why do you sound so hurt?! You said you WEREN'T here to try and influence me, remember! You literally said,

'Not at all.'"

"I'm really more disappointed that we didn't turn out to have a whole lot more in common than what we do. I'm very interested in 'third eye' mysticism and thought your essays were both fascinating and insightful." Joel shrugged.

Malang allowed his brow to furrow into a scowl. "I'm not at all ambiguous or cryptic about my submission to the Will of the Most-High in my blog posts. I've said nothing here standing before you that I didn't expound upon at length in my 'third eye' accounts. Should I believe that you thought I was only pretending to be an Abrahamic theist, or that you used your pagan mystic powers to somehow tell that I wasn't serious?" Malang smirked. "Which is it?"

"Listen, man, do you have the book and if you do, are you willing to sell it?"

"I do have Dr. Hessians' book. I am unlikely to sell it because it is both an influential work in my personal development and a rare first edition hardcopy I'd rather keep in my library. You know his estate heirs are selling a later edition soft cover version…"

"I know. I saw it." The two stared at each other for a few seconds. "Alright. Well, thank you for your time, Malang. Here's my card, okay? If you change your mind, please reach out."

The two exchanged their parting well wishes and Joel walked off. Malang noticed that the comedy duo of Bill and Fred were playing some kind of card game in their booth and apparently showed no interest in his encounter with the enigmatic Joel. Maybe they assumed he was just a customer and not worth their time, he thought. Margaret strolled Olivia up the aisle way towards his booth just after noon, a corned beef on onion roll meal from Malang's favorite local deli sitting on top of the stroller's sunshade.

"Hey, there, you two!" Malang sang, cheesing from ear-to-ear as much from the surprise lunchtime visit as he was pleased to see his wife's own gorgeous smile. He set his collection of #ADOS flyers to the side while Margaret prepared a spread for two. He told her about the Joel discussion.

"You're not going to sell it to him, are you?"

"Oh, no way. Plus I get the impression that he thought I was going to be a lot younger and more malleable maybe?"

"What do you mean? Like he wanted to mentor you?"

"Like he intended to try to exploit me in some way. Just a hunch."

"Well, you know you and your hunches."

"He lied a lot. Blatantly. When I pushed back,

he became deflated and confused. To be honest, the more I think about the whole thing the more irritated I get."

"You don't need to hold on to any of that now," Margaret scolded.

"You're right."

Malang cleaned up as his family moved along up the aisles to check out what the other flea market vendors had to offer. He watched as Margaret paused at a tattoo artist's spot, amused when her face started distorting in disgust. He couldn't tell if she was recoiling at seeing the work done or because the tattooist was doing it poorly.

"Are these for sell?"

"Yes, they are! Was there something you were interested in purchasing?" The clean-cut blond young man, he looked to be in his early twenties, pointed towards a print with a message that went particularly hard after the Democratic Party leadership.

"That one there is brilliant. Are you a Republican?" he asked hopefully.

"No, I'm registered as a Democratic at this time."

"Ugh!" the young man said with exaggerated disgust. "Come on! You have to free yourself from that plantation!"

"Yeah? I'm not really there for the 'plantation' part. I'm there because that's where the bulk of my identity group have their equity built in after several generations of loyalty to the party. As a political advocacy activist, it would easier to get my people to use their dormant voting power to strategize for wins within the party they are already loyal to, than it would be to get them to switch parties and shift their loyalties elsewhere."

"I guess that's true, but what has the Democrats really done for you?"

"A fair question, but that's my job as the activist to get my people organized so their party will get things done on their behalf, right? As difficult as it would be to push the Democratic Party machine in the direction we need, it would be a lot harder to do in the GOP."

"Why do you say that? That's not true," said the young man.

"No? What we need is our Reparations and a solid Black Political Agenda to make us finally economically equal with whites, the racial wealth gap closed. We need to be economically included in a wealth-building ownership class. Do you really think it would be easier to get THAT crowd…" Malang tilted his head in the direction of the deer hunter booth. "…to agree to that?" When the young man turned back towards Malang, his face was noticeably flushed.

"No, probably not," he said with a sheepish tone

in his voice. "But we do have many other benefits."

"Like what?" asked Malang skeptically.

"Peace of mind. Community. A sense of...!"

Malang interrupted. "Is any of that going to make me economically equal with whites and close the racial wealth gap?"

"No," the young man said after an uncomfortable hesitation. "Probably not."

"I'm not into the partisan, feel-good, smoke-n-mirrors showmanship of the modern political apparatus. I'm only interested in working the system to effectively get what I need from my government. That's all."

"You know," said the blond guy in a lowered voice. "Black people aren't the only ones who have problems, you know? My position is that we must let go of the past to move forward. I think this 'activism' thing is really just crippling you."

"That's an odd thing to say," Malang responded. "Literally every single identity group in the country has a dedicated political advocacy apparatus in place to ensure their people get the resources they require from the government to see their next generations better off. My group is the only one where when we rightfully proclaim we deserve no less than the same consideration, we receive comments like those in response. The Black American ethnic group has been struggling at an artificially imposed deficit for centuries and we deserve to be left alone to pursue our American happiness without rival groups trying to convince us to stay in a position more convenient to them. That's not right at all."

"I-I just think that clinging to all of that stuff just keeps you in that spot!"

"That doesn't make any sense. I'm in this spot because I've been terrorized and politically disenfranchised. My direct ancestors… the baby boomers… perfected the political advocacy model that literally every other group uses for their own economic come-ups while my group remains locked out of access. And THEN I have to hear people like you trying to talk me out of escaping that racist social engineering trap designed to hold me down."

"I don't believe that," said the blond guy with a scoff.

"Based on what?"

"You just live in a culture of playing victim."

Malang raised his chin up and eyed the young man. "Interestingly, 'playing the victim' is the con job that the women of your 'whiteness' identity perform all the time. They do their dirt and then cry victim, blaming an innocent or even fictitious Black American for the crime. For some reason you all have been pushing hard to project that mess onto Black Americans lately. Playing the victim' is your tool, not mine. The U.S. government was set up for me to advocate and lobby for group economic uplift, so it's pretty slimy to attempt to make me feel like I'm doing something wrong and unseemly by working the system as it was designed to be worked for my own people."

"If you're supposed to be somehow accusing me of racism, then that's absurd. I'm far from it."

Literally everything that my people need to finally be able to put the shadows of the past behind them, you feel it's your duty to talk us out of them and keep us in an exploitable state. That's definitely an act of racism to hold Black people down so your white group may maintain its economic dominance."

"All I want is for the people who treat others properly to get the best the culture has to give them," said the blond guy, choosing his words with care.

"That just sounds like you're trying to sneakily dance around your patented 'black-on-black crime' talking point to try and weave an elaborate tale of improperly-acting Black people who consequently wouldn't qualify to be treated properly according to the rules of your story time narrative. Meanwhile, in real life, it's the colluding cartels of immigrant groups who have consistently treated my people poorly for centuries, and their response to my protest is to tell me to just relax into it and shut up, like you have done twice now in this one visit."

"I'm not an immigrant. I was born…"

"Then you're an immigrant's kid. Or grand kid. You are immigrant-tied in some way or another and you lot have, as an interconnected political bloc, treated my group far worse than any common, desperate, poor class, Black street criminals have ever treated white people."

"Alright, this is getting stupid now."

"It was already stupid." Malang rubbed his face in what appeared to be an extended face palm remix. "This makes the second time inside the last hour where someone initially approached me being fake friendly, thinking they could manipulate me, who then turned mean when they discovered they couldn't."

The blond guy shoved his banking check card at Malang—his name was Brent Nieminen—who was confused at the gesture. Surprised, he realized Brent still wanted to purchase the print. Malang quietly and methodically ran the card through his reader, carefully wrapped the print and handed it over to his newest customer. "Thank you for your business."

"Yeah, yeah. Have a good one." Brent walked briskly back to his booth. He must have really enjoyed the message from his solid anti-Democratic Party worldview, Malang thought, to have bought it anyway despite the heated exchange.

"Maybe he bought it as his abrupt way of shutting me up," Malang muttered under his breath. He looked up and met Bill's eye across the aisle, who hurriedly looked away in clear irritation. Malang was of half a mind to go over there and stir up another argument, but his opponent's lack of weaponry held him back.

Twenty minutes later, the activity on their aisle started to pick up, a steady trickle of foot traffic—mostly composed of middle-aged and older white couples in groups pausing at each booth with seeming appreciative interest. When they got to Malang's booth, a similar pattern emerged: searching eyes would look at a selected print, the color would begin to rise in pale cheeks, eyes would dart over to Malang, a few more seconds of looking at the prints followed by a short noise of some sort, generally an emotional expression of disapproval. Amused, Malang for his part offered a friendly grin, trying to at least give the impression that he was open for the discussion if they were so interested. One gentleman stood closer than most, appeared to carefully study each print in kind. He glanced over at Malang with a full body sweep and then looked down at the table of ADOS

Advocacy Foundation flyers. He picked a few of them up – the Reparations focus for the American Descendants of Slavery ethnic group, the Black Political Agenda to include the other members of the immigrant-tied diaspora, the invitation to non-black groups (including whites) as allies to help ADOS guide the country towards living up to its highest ideals (finally). The man looked back up at the prints thoughtfully. He was tall, at least 6 feet 2 inches and appeared to be in his mid-60s, his hair a tidy short white underneath a soft cloth cap. He wore multiple layers of clothing – a medium jacket, button-down flannel plaid shirt with t-shirt underneath, showing that he was often cold despite the day's summer heat. Washed out blue jeans that hugged his thin legs floated above pink foam clogs in thick socks completed the costume.

"You're the artist?"

"Yes, sir."

"It's a shame to see someone so young be so angry."

Malang hunched his shoulder forward and stretched a bit, shaking his head slowly as he relaxed them. "Personally, I'm at peace in my faith and don't generally walk around 'angry' as you imply. I am informed on the history of United States race relations, the material that inspires my art activism. An objective study of the historical record reveals such wrong inflicted upon my identity group – the Black American former slave class – that it should invoke some kind of negative emotion response, assuming the one doing the study has any kind of basic human-level empathy for fellow human beings."

"What's your name?"

"I'm Malang."

"Ah. Pleased to meet you, Malang. I'm Ioan Tiplea. I see the logic in what you're saying, sure, but politics is a tricky thing. I think we can all agree it has mostly been a bad thing in society."

"I can agree that in my country, the political machine has been molested by the dominant political identity group to economically elevate them and their favored cliques, while being used to lock my people out of access."

"I'm sorry, what is your country again?"

"The United States of America," said Malang, with perhaps a bit more force than may have been necessary. Ioan paused for a beat.

"I mean, where is your family from?"

"I'm a member of the Black American ethnic group, Mr. Tiplea. This is the only country I know by design of my people's former slave holders. Our pre-Middle Passage ties were deliberately cut off to make us more effective chattel. Consequently, the eclectic African ethnic groups that made up the

American slave class were forced to mix and form a brand-new ethnicity. I am a proud member of that now 400-year-old brand new people. This is my home. My only home."

"I see." Ioan carefully pushed his thin-framed glasses up on his nose. "And you believe politics is supposed to do what for you now?"

"An odd question," said Malang with an eyebrow raised. "It's supposed to enable me to unify as a self-interested bloc to pressure elected representatives to provide the resources my people need from the government's enormous spending power for group uplift. The same that it does for every other identity group in the country."

"See, that's the problem right there: 'identity groups.' We're going to have to get rid of all of this divisiveness if we're going to really heal this country."

"I already mentioned the origins of the nation and its commitment to the free slave labor economy that built up its obscene great wealth primarily for the enjoyment of the descendants of the light-skinned European ethnic tribes. This is the well-documented legacy of the United states, of which it protects & coddles today. Are we now going to pretend 'divisiveness' started when my people again stepped forward to demand the economic inclusion to make us whole that has long been denied us after building the richest country on earth?"

Ioan put his hands up in a surrendering gesture. "I'm certainly not the one to say that the African-American hasn't been done regrettable wrongs. I'm not saying that. What I am saying is that the way to move forward in all of this involves healing everyone, not pausing to take several steps back towards the long-gone slavery days."

"White people keep saying stuff like that to me, as if they magically no longer understand the concept of Reparatory Justice in a civilized society. Meanwhile, you're the most litigation conscious people in the universe. You care very much for people doing right by you and insurance and carefully defined property lines and making sure you get EXACTLY what you have coming to you to honor agreed upon contracts, et cetera, et cetera, but when you happen to be in earshot of the American Descendants of Slavery demanding their equal share in our country – and I've been here far longer than ALL of you, Mr. Tiplea, immigrant's son – then you feel somehow obligated to preach at me in an suspicious effort to convince me I don't need to enjoy the full benefits of being an American. I cannot help but be offended by hearing this tripe over and over again, particularly by someone whose first words to me was to note that my work expressed anger. The same works inspired by the facts of history."

"It seems like you're getting upset now. It wasn't my intention to…"

"Should I not get upset? I told you that I advocate for my people, for what they NEED, you and people like you keep telling me I don't need that, to instead help you build things from your political goals. As if the various colluding groups of white people haven't already ben doing that for the last 400 years, but today it means 'we're healing as a nation.' I don't normally walk around with a chip on my shoulders, but if you insist upon pushing my buttons by trying to convince me that your political group's goals should force mine to the national backburner for another four centuries, how am I not supposed to get at least reasonably annoyed by the behavior? How would you feel if I did it to you? Well, not if I did it, since you obviously have zero respect for what I think, but if someone you actually respected did it to you?"

Ioan's face lit up. Malang couldn't tell if it was meant to be mocking him. "So, you respect me? Is that why I get you upset? That's a start, I guess."

"What I'm pointing out is that I give you, a stranger, a basic level of respect upon meeting you, a respect you did not afford to me since you casually felt it proper to crap all over the long-denied transformational politics my people need. Your GROUP consistently does that to me and it's insulting. Is that the type of 'unity' you're preaching while claiming my people are responsible for the 'divisiveness' you keep trying to pin on me?" Ioan wiped his mouth, looked up as if thinking of something meaningful to say. Finally he reached out and shook Malang's hand with a moist, weak grip.

"It's a pleasure to chat with intelligent people. You've given me a lot to think about and I thank you. Good luck with your work."

4

The Brief Trail

Dr. Carter Hessians placed his notes back into their labeled manila folders, straightened them neatly, and slid them into the soft brown leather briefcase compartment he designated public speaking notes to.

The crowd was decent enough at his "Discovering the Truth of the Road Towards Enlightenment" presentation at the gorgeous Mishigamaa State University campus in Potawatomi township, about 20 minutes outside of Chocolate City, but there had been no questions asked of him on the material and he decided to skip the Q&A portion set aside for him for fear of a bored embarrassment. So, he was surprised when he looked up ready to walk around the podium on his way back to his hotel to find a young man watching him with a look of genuine interest in his expecting face.

"Hi, Dr. Hessians," said the young man, tapping a large, permanent black marker against his right thigh. "They said that you weren't going to do the Q&A, but I'd hoped to ask a quick question or two before you left, if it's alright? Were you in a hurry?"

There was something familiar about him – Dr. Hessians assumed he was a student – and the elderly scholar, tickled to find himself in his 80th year of life, briefly tried to remember if this was the one who helped him find the Dr. Jesse Washington

Auditorium this morning…

"Ah. You're the young man who was manning the art booth I saw earlier. Very talented. What's your name."

"Thank you, doctor. My name is Malang. I'm very pleased to meet you. I'm just now discovering your work and found your presentation fascinating."

"Hm. Is that a fact?" said Dr. Hessians with a red-faced grin, failing to maintain a stoic, professorial aloofness he imagined was appropriate in the face of such unexpected flattery. "Well, then come along with me. We may as well grab a seat like civilized gentleman as we discuss the deeper mysteries."

The two stopped in the bookstore shoppe to grab some snacks (a packet of peanut butter crackers and a can of orange soda pop for the doctor and a comically large chocolate bar and flavored-milk drink for Malang) and then sat at a table close by the student lounge.

Malang downed half of his strawberry milk in a gulp from the small bottle and sat back in his seat. "I've never looked into the 'third eye' lore before, having just assumed it was pagan fiction. You hinted during your lecture earlier that it actually happened to you? Your third eye 'opened' as you put it?"

"Yes, it did. On a June afternoon in 1968. I will

never forget it."

"And what is your actual field of study? What do you have your doctorate in?"

"Physics."

"That's part of what's fascinating me about your talk. A physics scholar has publicly stated he has had a paranormal experience."

"I wrote a book about it."

"What's this book?"

"I titled it 'The Brief Trail.' It's a compilation of a series of lectures about my insights into the same topics you've heard. Within it, I've described the miraculous event in some detail." Dr. Hessians took a bite of his peanut butter cracker, studying Malang's facial expressions with focus. "The title references the point of the meditation practiced by the ancients, how the ritual is designed to get the adept to the verge of the altered state experience in as brief a time as possible. Without knowledge of this, people assume meditation is the only point of the ritual itself—meditating for the sake of meditating."

"Is your book still in print?"

"I believe I have an old copy in my bag here. It'll cost you a ten-spot."

Malang dutifully handed over a ten-dollar bill taken from that day's caricature earnings as the old man retrieved a thin, jacketed hard cover book from deep within his leather professor bag.

"Would you like me to sign it?"

"Please!"

Dr. Hessians pulled out a fountain pen with a flourish and did the needful. Malang looked it over briefly and sat it next to his candy. "I'm a subscriber to the Abrahamic faiths, so I am interested in the signs of the spirit. That's the nature of my interest. It seems like, based on a few hints and implications in your lecture, that you aren't a believer."

"No, I don't believe in those things. You have to understand that the 'third eye' was a profound experience, greater than anything I've ever read regarding those rather boorish organized religions. Over the years, I've come to believe that the Wisdom Eye itself is where my focus should be and I've dedicated myself to having it open again."

"By doing what?"

"With that same Ancient Egyptian technique of correct meditation. You see, one of my long-time hobbies I've picked up is the translation of the Egyptian hieroglyph. I discovered to my delight that the stele writings of the so-called pyramid texts contain detailed instructions for how to meditate and duplicate the initial sensation that heralds the 'third eye' event, the adepts theorizing that by making the environment so welcoming that the Wisdom Eye may deem one worthy to open."

"You discovered the meditation technique after you had the actual experience?" asked Malang.

"Yes."

"Then how did it open the first time?"

"Quite by accident of a sorts! I talk about it in the book," he said gesturing. "I sat down wrong when I plopped down into a wooden chair and rapped the base of my spine something awful… hurt like the dickens. At the moment of impact, my body was awash in an intense, tingling energy, my field of vision obscured by the all-encompassing otherwhere of the UDJAT Wisdom Eye of Heru! The 'third eye' portal appeared, set before me approximate 6-inches from my brow ridge. Such sights it showed me! And nearly as soon as it came upon me, it was gone."

"You knew what it was when it happened?" asked Malang, leaning forward with widened eyes.

"Ah! That's the thing! One of my other personal interests, since I was at least your age, has been the Tantric lore of Eastern Mysticism. I have studied meditation techniques far and wide in all their forms… a thousand, thousand books, papers, articles I've read over the decades. I learned in that one magical instant which of the authors had experienced the 'third eye' opening for themselves from a place of personal experience versus the ones who merely talked at the event from a low knowledge of speculation, generally just assuming that the rare individuals who knew what they were talking about truly were only speaking metaphor! There is metaphor in those old writings, absolutely. But it's the metaphor of someone describing the paranormal impossible with the poorly inadequate tools of mere men!"

"When you discovered the pyramid texts were talking about opening the 'third eye' it was part of...?"

"Oh, yes! I saw what they were talking about through the archaic symbolism! Where other more well-known interpreters were bogged down with flawed, literal-minded thinking, my experience showed me what the ancients were really telling us."

Malang found himself getting excited mostly from the scholar's ignited enthusiasm. "Okay, so when did you have your first meditation-induced 'third eye' opening?"

"I-I didn't. It only happened to me that once."

"During the accidental spine bump?"

"Right." Malang searched Dr. Hessians' face, his brow furrowing slightly. He looked down at his candy bar and started slowly peeling it open. After a thoughtful bite, Malang looked back up at the doctor.

"It sounds like you're saying that you searched

for mystic secrets your whole life, but rejected the revealed message of the One God out of hand. You were allowed a tiny glimpse into the unseen spirit, but instead of rethinking your position about the Abrahamic faiths, you went in the opposite direction and started to blasphemously deify the spiritual sign that pointed towards the One God." Dr. Hessians' face brightened red, a scowl beginning to distort his many wrinkles into a road-mapped mask. "I strongly suspect that any further 'third eye' openings are now closed to you because you failed that test."

"CHOOSING ANYTHING FROM THIS ILLUSORY WORLD, INSTEAD OF FINDING AND PREFERRING THAT PRECIOUS IMMORTAL STAR SIX INCHES BEFORE THE BROW IS IN FACT THE ULTIMATE ACT OF BLASPHEMY TO THE ONLY REAL GOD!!!" Phlegm and spittle flew from the distorted anger mask that was Dr. Hessians' smiling, excited face only moments before. Malang stood up and gathered his things, keeping a wary eye upon the doctor, who sat confused and deflated in his Members Only jacket, his eyes darting about at the curious faces looking in their direction.

"I didn't mean to upset you, doctor. That material is my own expertise and in a discussion of matters of faith and spirit, my contribution to an honest discussion can only be to compare your experience to what the Lord thy God revealed. The One God is not a part of the world of illusion; he's the One who created it so that we may recognize His handiwork, choose to be rightly-guided, believe and be grateful—perchance God may bless us with a glimpse into the wonders of the spirit along our journey to strengthen our faith. Since that kind of discussion is too much for you in light of the fact that you failed to recognize God's sign when it was gifted to you, I'll leave you to think your thoughts. Have a good day."

* * *

Malang seemed to feel the excitement of that long ago day all over again as he lied on his back in his marriage bed, his right elbow crooked over his eyes. Margaret nested up against his left side, the low buzz of her breathing seeming to be the perfect background noise to the tingle he felt. He had Dr. Carter Hessians' obituary stored somewhere in his files. Despite the crazy end to the crazy encounter, it was a day that opened many wonderful rabbit holes that ultimately served to make Malang a better believer in the One God, though some may consider that ironic. The enduring scripture of the ages assures the believers that the signs of God are to strengthen their faith, not to convert those who reject faith. In his readings, Malang at first assumed that meant those who didn't believe in spirit at all, but Dr. Hessians recognized his experience as real and at least managed to believe in the unseen, just not on the One God's terms... the only terms that matter. It's not likely that the doctor would have rethought his position just because he heard the admonishing words of a young Black American man whom he felt beneath him enough to scream at like a banshee at the top of his lungs.

Malang had asked Dr. Hessians about his own experiences practicing the pyramid texts' "correct meditation" instructions, but he now recognized from his own experience that the ancient rituals were only vain efforts to manipulate the unseen spirit to bend to the will of impatient men. Submitting to the One God, sincerely and diligently following the "Long Path" established by those believers of old who successfully followed the Straight Way is how one can be blessed to have the gifts of the spirit – including the legendary 'third eye' opening.

Following the sudden compulsion to shower, Malang slid out of bed, careful not to disturb his wife's adorable comfy, warm slumber.

He lathered up under the hot water stream, probing at the tinge of sadness he felt at the near certainty that Dr. Hessians died rejecting faith, dooming himself. He felt bad because the doctor's lecture represented a key milestone on his own spiritual journey that led to two amazing spiritual experiences that Malang would not have recognized were it not for his serendipitous decision to check out the oddly-titled speaking event, somewhat out of character for him considering in those days he usually sped right home after a long day at a caricature booth. As he dried off, Malang realized that he was focusing on the wrong thing – it is the One God who Plans. Truly of all those who plan, it is God who is the Best of Planners! Malang's chance meeting with Dr. Hessians – like everything else in reality – was God's manifested Will in action; the encounter had nothing to do with that old man who outsmarted himself out of the promise of Eternal Bliss. Moved almost to tears, Malang recited his prayer of gratefulness to his Lord as he got dressed, absently wondering if he should workout to get the excitement of the old memory off of him. Weird how he should feel so intense about…

Right when Malang finally realized that the excited tingle that had been building up in the last 10 minutes was actually the Serpent Fire of the Universe, his entire field of vision was filled with the *veil between realities*! Like the two times before, the 'third eye' portal was set before his brow about 6-inches away, its bright glow drawing in the full focus of Malang's conscious vision. For an unknown fraction of a second, he felt an overwhelming dread at what he mistakenly assumed was the worst thing he could imagine... he thought the Wisdom Eye was showing his ethnic group being returned to the shackles! Instead the vision he was shown – a sea of tens of millions of Black Americans, nearly all shades of melanin, each wrapped in the colors of Old Glory with their heads head high, as a parade of their rivals paid them tribute in the wealth they were due and saluted them as the nation's elite protected class, the admired of the world – was the ultimate in earthly success he could possibly ask for! After the political identity groups passed by, the 'third eye' showed him a succession of religious representatives, each genuflecting and paying tribute in respect and awe to the Black American throngs. For a scant few seconds (or so it seemed in the timeless 'otherwhere' as Dr. Hessians called it) the 'third eye' allowed Malang to zoom around as he liked to inspect the crowd in more detail, but it seized the control once more, zoomed out to show a long shot of the crowd, (Malang could see the Washington D.C. monuments in the background), and then the Wisdom Eye closed, his two physical eyes of First Sight staring out in startled gratitude at his bedroom, Margaret still breathing deeply from her undisturbed sleep. For an absurd moment he wondered how she could possibly sleep through all of that excitement and he grinned to himself at the goofy thought.

Malang got back into bed, his wife stretching out with a purring groan and then allowing herself to be pulled in close. As he replayed this newest 'third eye' opening over and over, mapping out its description in the blog post he planned to write, he assumed he wouldn't be able to sleep for the rest of the night, but he was wrong. Soon the couple's breathing was perfectly synced.

* * *

Lance Irons, MD, was a fourth-generation medical physician, his great grandfather having attained his doctorate at the Mishigamaa State University School of Medicine on the very short list of Negro freemen to have done so at the close of the 19th century. Upon attaining his degree, the eldermost Irons then moved his small family down to Peachbush, GA where the Irons clan have done very well for themselves, compared to the rest of the ADOS ethnic group, this century and a quarter. Like the three Irons before him, Dr. Lance also sat on the board of directors for the ultra-exclusive, non-collegiate fraternity known as "The Commission." His great grandfather being one of the original founders of this, the oldest fraternity for Black Americans, Lance Irons carried about him a degree of pride that expressed itself most obviously in the extra pep in his strut. As the only board member who kept his professional office at The Commission headquarters in downtown Peachbush, he was also the one most vexed concerning the tight budget and the significantly less than classy facility space. The first building, a former fire station purchased shortly after the fraternity's founding, was one of several set ablaze during a series of nasty race riots during the height of the jim crow era. Fortunately, they were able to secure another, an abandoned primary school in poor condition. The Commission's white handler base refused to sign off on more funds, forcing the board to come out of pocket for some of the most critical work, Lance footing more of it than anyone. Eventually, they were able to get it first up to code, and then slowly looking like a real professional headquarters of sorts.

Today, Lance sat at his desk, glaring intensely as he read the blog post his assistant forwarded to him. Lance had expressed to his peers on the board that it was his estimation that this "Flathill, Malang" was a threat to their primary mission of gatekeeping which professional Black Americans would be allowed to ascend into the upper echelons of accessibility to 'whiteness,' able to enjoy some degree of financial success and peace of mind away from the lesser crime-ridden Blacks. It was his strong opinion that the first two blog posts, in which Flathill claimed to have received some kind of mystic visions, flagged the man for being labeled a "Black Messiah," J. Edgar Hoover's term for those Black leaders capable of organizing the ethnic group to become effective economic competitors against the white aristocracy, threatening the entire white supremacist edifice with a new age flip of the power dynamic in the country. His concerns were dismissed since nothing in Flathill's profile suggested he had anything like the charisma or skill to command the attention of the people like a Malcolm X or Dr. Martin Luther King, Jr. In fact, his social media platforms featuring his 'social justice warrior' original imagery, barely registered a blip on any commercial lists. It was Lance's position that these mystic visions (it didn't matter if they were real or not, only that Flathill himself believed they were – what feats men could accomplish just with the positive power of the mind!) combined with the odd fellow's focus on an independent, anti-racism advocacy uncontrolled and unrefined through proper Assimilated Integrationist institutional vetting, represented a wild card that could not be allowed to run loose.

They refused to listen and now here is a third blog post; a third "mystic vision." The color rose up in Lance's proudly high-yellow face as he read the description of what reminded him of the vision of the Hebrew prophet Joseph – who dreamed of his family members bowing down to him in tribute within a cosmological allegory. Flathill appeared to be describing the Black American ethnic group receiving exactly what The Commission was established to prevent: the formal end of lineage-based systemic racism, i.e., the economic oppression of the American Descendants of Slavery. Obviously, such a nightmare could not come to pass. It would not only render The Commission obsolete, destroying over a century of proud tradition, but it would flip Western Civilization itself on its head! Who the hell would want a bunch of wealthy, uncivilized blackies running things? Not him.

After copy/pasting some key portions into a word processing application to print for his files, Lance determined that there was no need to put this matter before the board again… their refusal to see the threat seemed also otherworldly itself. He reached for his phone and grimly dialed a number.

"Yeah? Raye here."

"Good morning, Christian! I hope I didn't catch

you at a bad time? I hear something in your voice...?"

"Hey, Lance! No, I'm fine, I just had to cuss out a couple of these senior agents. You know how it is. I think I shouted myself hoarse is what you're hearing. How are you? How's Gail and the girls?"

"Oh, they're all great, doing great, them and their families. I tell ya, there's nothing like being a grandpop. Those little faces, you hear me? They can make your heart MELT, boy, I tell ya."

"Believe me I know. Listen, we need to get together again. It's been a while, right? That's crazy. Give me some time to deal with a little of this Bureau business, block off something on my calendar and you, Gail, Sally and myself can meet up at the cottage, right? How's that?"

"It sounds amazing."

"I'll bet. How can I help you, bud?"

"Christian, I need to report something in for COINTELPRO under the 'Black Messiah' file. It's urgent."

"Really?"

Lance explained to the F.B.I. Director Christian Raye his concerns around the Flathill file. Director Raye sat silent on the phone during the whole narrative. Occasionally, Lance could hear the scratch of a pen on paper, or a short flurry of tapping on the keyboard. He started to suspect the

Director was zoned out, lost in his Bureau world and he expected the same blow off he received from The Commission board of directors.

"You did good, Lance."

"You... you think so? I mean, I didn't really want to jump the gun on something that turned out to be... I mean, who is this guy, right?" Lance wiped at the light perspiration formed on his brow. "It's not like he has a lot of fans or whatever."

"Are you now trying to talk me out of what you tried to concern me with?" Director Raye said with an amused chuckle. "I said you did good. There's a whole lot at stake here. History has shown that it's the things you don't see, that don't really seem like much at all, that can get you. What did Goliath think when little David showed up with his slingshot? The kid was a joke! A gnat! Then the invincible giant was dead with his head cut off and little David was king of a nation, right? Well, not on my damned watch. Lance, you did good. It's our job to protect the empire and we do that by scrutinizing the little things that our big guns can't or won't see. Yeah, we'll get together soon. Give Gail and the girls my love."

"I will! Thank you, Christian."

"No, thank you. You're a great man, Lance. You take care."

"Good bye."

"Bye."

* * *

A tall, dark chestnut-brown man stepped out of the taxi cab when it pulled up in front of the light grayish tan, low-rise office building in Washington D.C. Waiting for the driver to return his change, the slightly overweight man put on his dark glasses, musing that walking up to the J. Edgar Hoover Building was the best (and only) thing he liked about this city. "Don't go far away. I don't plan to stay," he told the driver.

"Sure thing."

The man slowed down a little as he approached the automatic doors, annoyed they didn't respond in time to match the quickness of his stride. After the obligatory x-ray security search, he approached the receptionist desk.

"The directory is waiting for you, Special Agent Konde. You may go on up."

"Well, well, well," sang Director Raye. "Philip Konde. If I didn't know any better, I'd say you didn't like coming to my wonderful city."

"It's okay, I guess." The two shook hands and the director motioned for the agent to have a seat in one of two black leather chairs sitting in front of his desk. Special Agent Konde made a show of straightening his tie, smoothing the back of his slacks on the black suit the director mirrored, and plopped down, crossing his legs. Director Raye shook his head.

"You're not that cool. You really look like you watch too much television."

Special Agent Konde shrugged and got right to business. "I read the file. I think this 'Malang Flathill' nobody is just that: A NOBODY. He's a troll and a kook. He's not even that good of an artist. The only noteworthy thing about him is his decision to promote the work of Moore and Carnell—the two behind this #ADOS group—and people aren't even taking him seriously with that really."

"Well, what do you propose?"

"I want to assemble a team – I happen to have just the crew – and we'll go after this ADOS instead. That's where the danger is. The idea that the blackies will come together politically and get the government to make them a competitive protected class is a no-no. Why you're even thinking about this other dude is beyond me."

"You're right about the ADOS thing. We already have people on that for exactly that reason, but if you want to join that force and add your talents to it, then the more the merrier. You're wrong about the other guy though. The religious component of the whole thing… you can't underestimate that stuff. The 'fire of faith' in the minds of men can move mountains if they believe enough, and these visions this guy is claiming—if that talk just happens to ignite these people under ADOS, it could spread like the meteorite rise of Islam did. Like overnight! The next thing you know, they'll not only have the Reparations they want, but they're also our damned bosses. I sure as hell don't want that."

Special Agent Konde remained unconvinced. "If you say so. I think your own religious leanings…"

"I actually don't have any," Director Raye interrupted.

"Well, Director, there's something there in you that's being triggered by his whole shtick. I see it when you talk about it." The agent watched his boss carefully. Director Raye allowed the professional to study him for a few more seconds and then flashed a grin. "Keep your secrets," Konde said, returning the grin. "I'll fly on up to Chocolate City and pay the weirdo a visit. I'm going to troll the troll and make him doubt his own name."

"Okay. Do your best. I'll admit I feel better with you on it."

"That sounds like a compliment!"

"Get out of here. Get to work."

* * *

The annual Africa-for-Africans World Festival usually matched the crowds at the Jazz Festival and this year was no exception. Also using the Heath Galleria space near the Chocolate City downtown walkway, Malang Flathill found himself on the other side of the plaza than he was last fall. By now, word of the ADOS movement had spread and Malang found himself in more informative discussions helping direct Black Americans towards the ADOS Advocacy Foundation's website for more information as to how they, too, could add their talents and skills to the growing body. There were no white supremacist leaning ideologues, like the deer hunters he shared booth aisle space with at the Cyprus Trade Center that time, but there were a lot of Black immigrants who seemed equally as hostile. Malang was taken aback; was this not THE Africa-for-Africans World Festival, where the ideals of "Pan-Africanism" were supposed to be promoted as a good thing? Well, didn't that mean that the diaspora was expected to support the efforts of their fellow Black people's enfranchisement and confrontation of their own government over what they were owed? The push back was baffling.

"You act like you were the only people who ever had to fight the veils of white racism!" said one angry African character. "You should be ashamed!"

"I'm not saying any such a thing," Malang responded. "I'm saying that my group has a very specific grievance with our own U.S. government tied to our own ethnic group's unique lineage & heritage. We're demanding a specific Reparations program tailored towards us for the damage specifically done to us in our country. I don't see what the disconnect is here."

"There is no 'disconnect!' There's only your selfish xenophobia!"

Malang thought to detect the root cause of the issue.

Greed.

Big money was being discussed and it didn't matter if it had anything to do with this guy or not, he wanted his hands in it. "Look, I'm not saying your own group wasn't discriminated against by either your own colonialist era oppressor, or even in some way by the U.S. depending on when you showed up or whatever. In any event, if you conclude that your own specific identity group is also owed reparations, then you need to establish your own unique grievance separate from the ADOS one which has noting to do with the diaspora. The ADOSAF organization does have a wider Black Political Agenda with items that do include you as the Black U.S. immigrant class, but our Reparatory Justice claim 'is sacred' as Yvette said."

The guy continued to cuss and rant over whatever imagined monies he feared he wasn't going to get from something he wasn't even remotely entitled to, until eventually Malang was forced to call over one of the Heath Galleria patrolling officers to come remove him. Among the crowd of onlookers, a few turned to look at Malang in derision, to which he lifted up his hands.

"What?"

"That was uncalled for! We Black people have to learn to come together!" said one, wearing a throwback "X" cap from a popular 1990s Black film.

"Well, my disenfranchised Black ethnic group trying to come together with enfranchised Black immigrant groups turned out to be an abysmal failure. Coming together over racial phenotype isn't a thing for us… that's the white man's invention designed to economically empower him at my expense. If we are going to come together, it should be as independently strong, interconnected political identity groups in which what we will each get out of the union is clearly defined upfront. Otherwise, as the pass half century has demonstrated, the Pan-Africanist kumbaya has only made my people the exploited mule for you all's come ups. No more of THAT, thanks."

Malang patiently put up with being called "xenophobic" a bit longer (barely), as the two tag-teamed in trying to convince him that "coming together" somehow involved the Black American remaining disenfranchised, wealthless and a despised bottom caste so that Black immigrants could not only use civil rights era laws and policies for their own politico-economic elevation, but so that they could ultimately erase the history of the American Descendants of Slavery altogether and replace it with a fabricated false narrative where Black immigrants built the country instead. From the way they passionately screamed it, Malang gathered that they were somehow actually expecting him to accept this idea as a plus for HIS group.

He shook his head, took in a deep breath, and refocused his attention upon the core aspects of the ADOS movement message.

"The problem the Black American is dealing with," said Malang patiently. "is that we've been artificially impoverished, starting from slavery, but continuing through the 150 yrs into the now. Every effort to make it right along the way was immediately sabotaged, countered. When we took a step forward, we were immediately pushed two or three steps back... all the while the white dominant identity group have amassed more and more wealth plundered from us to add to their passed down inheritance hoards. Today, white people control $140 trillion of the national household wealth, while the American Descendants of Slavery only control an abysmal sliver of that in illiquid baby boomer assets and pensions."

A mummer from the crowd. Malang frowned as he started to catch the term "financial literacy" floating about. The temptation to roll his eyes was so strong his right eye began to spasm. He rubbed it with a knuckle.

"What we need is that financial literacy!" said a light-skinned older gentleman right on cue. He wore a sweater, styled after one popularized by a famous comedian's 1980s tv show, over a white button-down shirt, his hands in the pockets of his creased khakis. "That hustle and grind is what will get us out of the poor house. Do the work!"

"Negative. You're not going to 'hustle & grind' your way to economic equality with a guy who is unfairly hoarding $140 trillion, that's insane. The hustle & grind without politics means the lineage-based racial wealth gap will continue to widen. It must be combined with the government's enormous spending power leveraged on your behalf. That's how that one got those trillions, with politics and policies. The Black American ethnic group has been deliberately locked out of access to capital, credit & wealth-building ownership for centuries as a group, but we've always had talented hustlin' & grindin' folk doin' their thing, even during the heights of both slavery and jim crow. That's where all of those successful Black communities and towns that were burned to the ground came from, right? Here in the faux 'Integration' Age, our ideological foes love propping up individual outliers as false-proof that the group doesn't need the transformational politics deliberately withheld since Lincoln was shot. We know how to hustle & grind, that's how we've survived this far... that's not the issue. The issue is thriving with group uplift, which is what politics is all about."

The previous crowd mummer had now taken on a tone of approval and general positivity, with many stepping forward to take away copies of the printed ADOS materials. As Malang fielded some questions, directing curious faces towards the primary source of his talking points—the tonetalks and BreakingBrown online video sharing platform channels of Antonio Moore and Yvette Carnell respectively—as well as to the ADOS Advocacy Foundation website, he looked up and caught the eye of a gentleman standing along the other side of the walkway. The man was tall, at least 6ft 5 in, with chestnut-toned dark brown skin. He wore a white t-shirt/short set, an expensive pair of gym shoes, and wasn't at all shy about public bedazzlement as he was practically draped in jewelry. When he saw he had Malang's attention, he took off his expensive designer sunglasses, a diamond stud danced in the early afternoon sun in each ear. He approached with the awkward confidence of someone out of his natural element and cosplaying to the image he saw in his mind. The man leaned in to give Malang some dap.

"What's up, bruh. I like your hustle, y'know? That's what's up," said the guy, scanning the booth space and nodding in approval.

"Thanks," said an amused Malang. "Appreciate it." The guy directed his scan towards Malang, looking him up and down and then directing a quick pointing finger at him.

"You're Malang Flathill, right? Yeah, I recognize you from your blog. Interesting stuff." Malang figured his mouth must have been hanging open or something, because the gentlemen glanced over at him and snickered. "Yeah, I know you. That's right. I've been following your work for a while. I've seen you around. Thought I'd walk up today and speak this time, like I got some manners." The two shook hands and exchanged a light, formal greeting. Getting right to the chase, the new visitor asked Malang a penetrating question.

"Yes, the 'third eye' opening events were very real, Phillip. They were entopic experiences, so I can't imagine how I would or could prove they were real with any instrumentation I would know about."

"So, you admit they could be something other than real?"

"No."

"No?!"

"No," repeated Malang with firmness. "It definitely happened, but it happened for me. My job is to share the insights gleaned—which you've read on the blog posts—but I can't share the experience no more than you can share your dream experiences."

"The main difference there is that we both know that dreams aren't real though!" said Phillip in triumph.

"I guess it depends on how you are defining 'real' in that case."

"Are you serious? I dreamed about a puppet show in the clouds that rained down paintball pellets whenever they were noticed. That's the last dream I remember. I can confidently say that it wasn't real." Phillip snorted with a gesture suggesting that Malang may be a little touched.

Here we go, thought Malang. He's one of those. Started off friendly and pleasant and then turned, revealing some hostile hidden agenda. As Malang raised his chin preparing to respond, he noticed Phillip's face change in an instant and he began watching Malang with a cool wariness. Whoever this guy is, thought Malang, he's skilled in reading body language.

"I would say that the dreams represented real messages from your subconscious. I don't think it wise to simply dismiss them as trivial mind farts or what have you. Some dreams really are predictive, true glimpses of second sight into the unseen spirit."

"You can't prove that though."

"I don't need to prove it."

"What?"

"I don't need to prove matters of spirit, Phillip. We obviously don't have the instrumentation to study things like 'mysteries of abstract conscious phenomena' the same way we could study animal anatomy, so why deliberately cripple ourselves with the odd assumption that that's the only way to study anything at all? That's not an intelligent approach to life."

"Yeah, well, if I can't touch it, taste it, feel it, hear it, see it, then guess what? It ain't real."

Malang shook his head. "Faith and belief are very real tools in the human life kit."

"That we need to get rid of!"

"No. Even in science we use those tools. They are vital to scientific progress. Without faith, inventors like the Wright brothers would have never pushed through nigh-endless failures to put together their flying apparatus prototype, let alone actually test it."

"That wasn't faith!"

"Of course it was," Malang smiled confidently. Without the BELIEF that it could be done with the technology they had available, without full commitment to the faith in their idea, they would have given up before it was a success." Phillip watched him and grew stony-faced. Malang wondered what was going on behind his eyes. "That level of faith is small potatoes. It's a big universe. An even bigger reality. To conclude that there is nothing in existence except what the puny human being of earth is able to grasp is not sound thinking."

Phillip remained silent for almost 30 seconds and eventually looked away. Malang wanted to say, "Take your time," but was reluctant to sacrifice the moment for a cheap gag. To his surprise, Phillip made an apology and excused himself, promising to see him around. It seemed to Malang that he had initially settled in for the long haul… "I got time," as the kids say. He guessed not.

Special Agent Konde didn't want to admit that he was a little shaken; that would force him to recognize the uncomfortable feeling of cognitive dissonance as a big portion of his worldview (he didn't realize exactly how big until just now) crumbled apart right in his face. His parents were immigrants from Tanzania, and they raised him strictly in the Abrahamic faiths. Since he was a small boy, Special Agent Konde thought the whole song-n-dance was a load of malarkey—how come they couldn't see it was all a joke?—and his being able to see that while no one else seemed to, made him smarter than almost everyone he knew and/or met throughout his life. So he thought. But now he had actually encountered a theist capable of confidently pushing back against some of his best stuff and Special Agent Konde found himself… frightened. What if he was actually wrong about everything? What if the logic wasn't really on his side, but on the other side, and he just never encountered someone capable of walking the materials down logically on Special Agent Konde's level before?

Maybe the weirdo wasn't really a troll.

Special Agent Konde decided he had let himself get spooked for no reason just because the guy turned out to be more competent than expected. Director Raye may have been right about him being a "true believer" as they call it. How could that be though, he thought, when through all reasonable conclusions he could come up with, that spiritual mumbo-jumbo had to be a fiction. So, how could this cat be so confident holding onto an illusion? He seemed smart enough—he certainly spun Konde!—so how could he not know, somewhere deep inside of him no matter how much he told himself he was a true believer—that the shit just wasn't real?!

He decided to merely double-down on his technique. Special Agent Konde has always successfully planted a seed in these smart theist types and they would, more often than not, end up turning atheist at some point. If you're a smart theist, then logic is your weakness. If you can't logic it out, then your faith will eventually unravel. This Malang was no different, just a higher grade of opponent, that's all. Special Agent Konde will just have to up his own game to find the dude's natural weak point, but it was there. It's definitely there.

* * *

That night, Malang described the mysterious Phillip to Margaret, particularly his seemingly uncanny ability to read his body language in a way that seemed like he had read his mind.

"Like, he could tell the moment I saw through his charade and it visibly shook him. We were basically playing chess… or poker, you know? Like we could see each other tells, but he was definitely more put out over it than I felt."

"It sounds like you two were the best artists at your high schools, and then met each other in art college," said Margaret, carefully brushing Olivia's hair into a tiny bun sitting on the top of her head. The family sat on the floor at the foot of the couple's bed, several baby toys strewn about, a small basket of haircare products and tools leaned against Margaret's left hip. Malang let out a hearty guffaw that startled the baby. Before she could cry, he quickly lied down in front of her and looked up into her face as she sat between her mother's legs. Her face immediately stopped its distortion attempt and reversed course into a smile.

"There she is!" Malang sang, cooing in time to Oliva's giggles. "It's funny because I did have that exact experience."

"Yup. I know. You told me," said Margaret in a nasal monotone, sincerely hoping her husband wasn't about to tell that story again.

"They used to have me do year books, posters for the dances, everything. I even drew the…"

"…comic strip for the school paper," Margaret finished. "Yup."

"And then when I went to art school…"

"Chuck Winters. Yup."

"Maaaan, ole Chuck Winters. That's right. We were the only…"

"…two Black students in the whole school. Yup. Sooooo, about this guy at the festival today, was he an artist, too?"

A few moments of silence from Malang as his quiet smile and dancing eyes gave away his reliving his undergrad with whatever geeky, artsy-fartsy adventures he was thinking about with "ole Chuck Winters." Margaret smirked as she fastened an orange barrette on the baby's little bun.

"Huh? Was he an artist?" repeated Malang as he rejoined the family. "I can't say. We didn't talk about that. He just mentioned that he was familiar with my work."

"The day itself went well though?"

"Oh, yeah. It was a great crowd. A lot of engagement. A better positive energy over-all than what I remember the last time I was at the Galleria."

"Okay, good."

"There was this one time, when Chuck Winters sketched out this tug-of-war piece, right? And I..."

Margaret surrendered with an audible groan ("oh, my God...") and glared at Malang during the duration of his 15-minute boring story.

* * *

"Well, hey! Good morning, Prophet Malang!" Malang looked up from straightening the stacks of ADOS flyers to see Phillip walking towards him. On this second of three Africa-for-Africans World Festival days, the grinning visitor was wearing a navy-blue t-shirt/short set, matching expensive gym shoes and the same entire jewelry store of bedazzlement as yesterday. Phillip seemed to follow his eyes and unconsciously reach for the 4 or 5 bracelets on his left wrist.

"Good morning, Phillip. Please don't call me that. I'm not a prophet. I make no such claims."

Special Agent Konde looked genuinely confused at this. "What? Are you serious? I thought that was the whole point?"

"The whole point of what? I'm a committed Abrahamic theist, not an aspiring cult leader or whatever. My goal is to enjoy my mansion in paradise, not piss off the One God by telling the people anything I have no right to say. The formal *Age of the Prophets* is behind us; what they left is the written Word of God they preached. All I am authorized to do is what we are all authorized to do: study to show my own self approved, remind the people of the revealed message and share my insights with my group in fellowship that we all may prosper both in this world and in the next. That's it. If the Christ (*peace be upon him*) said he didn't bring any new laws, then I sure as heck didn't. I'm just me."

"Well, I sure can't tell. You make a lot of fantastical claims in those blog posts." Special Agent Konde pointed quizzically at one of Malang's steel folding chairs and was given the welcoming go ahead to take a seat.

"No, all I did was describe what happened, what I saw to a degree. Humans have limited spiritual encounters all the time, like I mentioned briefly yesterday. We're always catching brief glimpses of the unseen spirit in some way or another. They don't have to be as dramatic as the 'third eye' opening events, but they happen. We've trained ourselves to dismiss, ignore, or just explain them away as something else. I think that's a mistake. What we all need to do is keep a journal of these events for the human record, so we can study them to see the emerging patterns. That's as close to the scientific 'proof' you insisted upon as we're likely to get, I think. That might even change depending on what those patterns could show us, but right now, collecting the data should be a huge part of human culture. I'm sure in some places in the world it is… and in the distant past."

Special Agent Konde sat hunched forward, his elbows on his thighs, looking at the ground between his feet and listening silently as Malang talked. Malang was disappointed that Phillip wasn't still studying him – he had intended to take the challenge and be conscious of his own facial tics & tells with a novel and game opponent, but the opponent no longer seemed as game as before.

"Are you alright?" Malang asked.

"Oh. Yeah. I'm just listening. You seem to know your stuff, I'll give you that," said the agent, still looking at the floor. "My issue with it all is that you put so much emphasis on stuff that's written in some old, man-made book."

Malang frowned. "Is that where you want to go? I thought you came to bring it. I'll admit to disappointment."

"I mean, look…"

"Phillip, are you really sitting there making disparaging comments about books while trying to project intelligence at me? Somehow you've seemed to have missed the fact that knowledge is recorded in books. It's a great innovation really, yet Phillip here apparently thinks it's stupid. This is you desperately trying to get a rise out of me by taking a position that shows you in a poor light."

"That's not what I said."

"It is what you said. Perhaps it isn't how you intended it to come across to me, or maybe it is how you intended it to come across and you thought I'd fall for some silly trap. But you know what? I'll play. Let me help you: What's wrong with human scribes recording the revealed message of the One God in books for the benefit of greater humanity? Why is that a horrifying thing in your mind?"

"Because it's not from a god."

"Based on what?"

"It's just not."

"So, you have faith… you BELIEVE… that sacred scripture didn't actually come from God. Well, I do believe it was revealed by God, and since I'm the one with the tangible item of that belief in my hands—the Book that entire human civilizations were built around, numerous systems and institutions designed around the concepts it instructs that have lasted throughout the ages—that means I win. By contrast, the fruit of your belief is a literal nothing at all, while the fruit of my belief is the enduring scripture passed down through the generations since time immemorial. That sounds like a sign from God to me, but of course I'm biased towards logic, reason and truth."

"Well, it's a sign from which god then? Huh? There's something like 9,000 religions, so which god is supposed to be the right one?"

"There is only One God."

"Could've fooled me."

"That's part of why He revealed the Book to humankind… to tell us who He was, who we were, to explain our relationship to the unseen spirit, provide the criterion of right & wrong and warn us of the coming of a Terrible Day… and JUDGMENT. He also explained over and over again that the idols wayward humans created were but vain fictions and to knock it off so that we may prosper. What's missing in the record of literature are any formal answers to the One God's revelations by any rival 'deities.' The One God remains undefeated in this regard and He said, definitely, that there is no god but He. Glory be to the One God! The Cherisher and Sustainer of the worlds!"

Phillip muttered something with unmistakable passion that Malang didn't hear.

"What did you say?"

"IT CAN'T BE REAL BECAUSE I DON'T WANT TO GO TO HELL!" Phillip shouted. He stood up to almost his full height, stooped forward a little as if in a defensive posture, his face working like he was struggling to control the ugly cry flood gates. "I'm 41 years old, bruh. I've spent my whole life talking shit on that stuff, but if I turned out to be wrong…?!" He shook his head and wiped a hand over his face. "I cursed my own father out when I left home because I thought he was a superstitious fool! You're making me doubt. I thought I had it all figured out… that I just KNEW!" Malang watched him with a stoic face. "Why would a loving God put people He made in hell forever because they were wrong and made a MISTAKE, bruh?! Tell me that!"

"God is God," Malang replied. "It is written, 'I am that I am,' He said to Moses (*peace be upon the prophet*). God is all-powerful, all-knowing and does whatever He feels like doing without restriction. No one can challenge Him—is this not His reality to do with as He likes? This is what it means to be GOD. The One God set up the rules for His reality according to His own whims and told you upfront what His expectations were and revealed what you needed to do and avoid in order to win at life according to His established criteria. Who cares what you think about it? Who cares that you think forever is too long for the Ultimate Punishment? Did God ask you? Do you have the power to make Him change His mind?"

"I hope there is a Judgment Day so I can tell god what I think about him!"

"You're being silly. The full trial of the Day of Judgment is for the believers, not for those who rejected faith. What would be the point of line-iteming your record of deeds if you couldn't even pass the most basic eligibility requirement to believe in the One who made you? No. God will let the heavenly host handle His light work and won't even acknowledge He notices you're there. An angel will roughly seize you, drag you to the event horizon of the roaring Pit and fling both you and your worthless record of deeds in head first. God will never think about you again. EVER."

Incredibly, Phillip's swelling, red-rimmed eyes

welled up with tears and he clumsily excused himself.

5

The Dark Web We Weave

An hour after listening to Special Agent Konde explain, in so many uncharacteristic words, how he was not doing well against this Flathill guy, F.B.I. Director Christian Raye stood at the 5th floor window of his office in the J. Edgar Hoover Building feeling very disturbed.

He sipped from a short glass of brownish-gold liquor, watching the Washington D.C. pedestrians moving along in their lives, thinking their own thoughts.

Director Raye had never heard him unravel like that, not in the 18 years he had known Special Agent Konde. He didn't really know where to put it. He had read the agent's file, of course. A precocious child of deeply religious parents, he'd had it together from day one. Konde seemed like the very last person to breakdown crying over some religious experience. Not the type of Kooksville religious experience that Flathill was supposed to be going on about, but an experience of losing a debate with a certified religious nutcase. Director Raye unconsciously blinked rapidly as he struggled to wrap his mind around a celebrated senior agent meeting his match in such a mundane manner that appeared to break him. He considered calling this in to HR and putting Konde on suicide watch.

The director walked back to his desk and pulled up a folder full of contact files. Slowing scrolling through each, one-by-one, he came by a name that made him pause thoughtfully. He clicked it open, revealing a puffy-faced older gentleman with an unkempt shock of graying mouse-brown hair. The photo was labeled "Wertheim, Pat Benjamin." Even though Konde held a master's degree in criminal justice and was undeniably whippet smart, Director Raye thought, he wasn't what you'd call an intellectual, *per se*. He wasn't a philosopher, continuously tweaking his perspectives in a sincere search for truth on this spirituality stuff. Once Flathill poked holes in his one-trick pony road show, he couldn't recover, but an actual intellectual with a flexible mind would be able to recover, Raye thought.

* * *

Pat Wertheim didn't intend to become a successful podcaster. When he started out on his career path as a career academic, entrepreneurship was the furthest thing from his mind. Pat was more than happy to live the tenured university life just writing, teaching and socializing.

Then evolution happened. Evolution changed everything.

A series of events that Pat would have never predicted, plunged his life into chaos. He was forced to adapt. One day, while giving a lecture on evolutionary biology, Pat casually mentioned a popular former sports star who had publicly transitioned to another self-identified gender role. He thought the joke was at least mildly funny in a self-indulgent way, but the 60+ stony faced students that greeted him felt otherwise. Wild accusations started to be tossed about, incredibly with his name attached. Pat's half-hearted efforts to damage control (surely, all of this wasn't really happening…?) seemed to make things worse and the next thing he knew…

…he was canceled.

No tenure. No job. He was ruined.

The termination letter from the University of Las Californias was coldly impersonal; the faculty refused to take his calls, to answer his emails. Colleagues he'd known for years were monosyllabic and wouldn't even look him in his eye. Not one to take defeat lying down, he fought back with his voice and the power of the pen. Angry blog posts turned into press releases and the next thing he knew, Pat was not only on a lecture circuit describing the crazy thing that was happening to him, but he was now being treated like an arch-villain by his own darling political left! Absurd terms like "transphobic," "intolerant," and "misogynist" (WHAT?!), were leveled at him in the liberal popular press.

Incredulously—fortunately—he wasn't alone. About a dozen or so other career intellectuals were being attacked for not kowtowing to this sociopathic feeding frenzy that seemed to have no point to it at all other than some bizarre, pro-anarchist insanity. The group met for support and to strategize an effective plan to reclaim their lives and at the end of it...

...the "Rational Murky Net" was born. A fiercely defiant, loosely-connected group of public intellectuals resigned to living on the edge of the accepted ideas of the sheeple mainstream, the members of RMN vowed to dedicate their skills to defend not only their freedom of speech, but the holy structure of Eurocentric, white male dominated Western Civilization with their last breath!

To a man, they each started podcasts, subscription membership platforms and branded merchandise stores to go along with their public tag-teams in highly-popular lectures and friendly (but heated & opinionated) debates. It didn't take long for the rebellious group to become a new segment of the celebrity set, using their individual and combined RMN platforms to dramatically influence the national discussion and become independently wealthy in the process.

Today, Pat had a big day planned with two podcast interviews, one featuring a fellow RMN member and the other a former university colleague who wants to formally apologize in front of Pat's audience. He snickered wryly while straightening up the studio for his guests, thinking the old coot just wants some of Pat's new celebrity magic to rub off on him, maybe even use it to catapult his own independent entrepreneurial adventure. He didn't mind since the guy was all about supporting the same virtues that the RMN swore to protect. The more the merrier, he thought. The phone rang and he muttered an irritated curse.

"This is Pat."

"Hey, buddy. We need you." A hard stone immediately appeared in Pat's stomach and he almost gave away an audible groan.

"Wh-who…?" he started to ask, but he knew who it was.

"It's Raye."

"Ho. Lee. Shit. I'm sorry. Was that not professional enough? Let me try again. Hi, Raye! It's been a minute!"

"It has. I have a mission for you. It's urgent."

"Well, if it's urgent then I have to do it, right?" asked Pay with as much annoyed sarcasm as he could project. "What is it?"

"I have an overconfident blackie who thinks he's the second coming. He's a little too uppity for his own good, if you get me. I need someone of your intellectual stature to reach in and smack 'em around a bit, knock 'em down a few pegs. Really make him feel it."

"Alright," said Pat warily. Could this really be all? "Is that it?"

"Break him. Really humiliate him. If he develops a drinking problem and commits suicide afterwards, that will be great."

"Wow. Who is this guy?"

"Check your email." Still irritated at the interruption, Pat nevertheless did as he was told. He opened an encrypted file, read its introductory contents, followed the link to a blog – some kind of social justice, blackie artist, spirit guru…? – and read through the short essays. Pat sat back in his chair frowning.

"So, you want me to give this weirdo nobody a spot on my platform? Are you serious? You realize there's no such thing as bad publicity, right? I have half-a-million subscribers compared to his, what? Seventeen? If I put him on my show, he'll just gain sympathy fans."

"I want you to humiliate him and chase him off the path he's currently on. I don't care where you do it at, just get it done." The phone connection dropped with deliberate finality. Pat continued holding it to his ear for a few moments as he skimmed back over the third blog post.

* * *

Malang held Olivia on his lap, bouncing her around on a knee as she delighted in hearing her own droning hum flutter to the motion. He sat at his desktop computer, typing in the data from this past weekend's festival with one finger. The "Dawdle in the Backstreet" event was a local favorite with an interesting crowd and he seemed to have spent the entire weekend actively engaged. He took a quick break and explored the notifications and activity on his various social media sites, his eyebrows raised when he saw what appeared to be a connection request from an infamous celebrity figure that, as far as Malang was concerned, he had little in common with.

"Bae? Come here for a second." Olivia reached up for her mom to pick her up when Margaret stepped into her grab zone. Margaret gently rubbed the baby's head as she leaned over Malang's shoulder to see what he was gesturing towards. "Do you see that?"

"Uhhh... what does he want?" she asked confused.

"That's exactly what I was asking."

"Well, what are you going to do?" Margaret picked up Olivia instinctively, who immediately started reaching towards her father.

"I'm not convinced I should do anything." Malang looked at the name for a few beats longer and then clicked away.

* * *

A couple of days later, Malang received an email soliciting a response. He noticed the name of Wertheim's "Black Sheep" company brand in the customized address. Malang sighed and slowly stroked his goatee for almost a full minute before he leaned forward and clicked the email open.

> *Greetings Mr. Flathill,*
>
> *I've been made aware of the thought-provoking claims you've described on your blog and would like to formally invite you to an interview on The Black Sheep Podcast. It's my understanding that you are not a man to shy away from a serious discussion and I think both of our audiences/subscribers would enjoy the show to our mutual benefit. Please respond with the date/time that works best for you. We would love to have you.*

Sincerely,
Pat Wertheim

Malang re-read the email and then clicked the Reply button.

Dear Mr. Wertheim,

Thanks for reaching out. I do not mind debating, or discussing the concepts I champion on your show, but in order to agree to do it, I need your assurance that I would be able to explain what #ADOS/ADOS Advocacy Foundation are, who their co-founders Antonio Moore and Yvette Carnell are, and be able to promote the political unification and pro-Reparations agenda of the Black American former slave class to your audience, giving those with an interest the ability to hear about this worthy subject matter and pursue provided links for more information. This would have to be a component of what actually gets aired. If not—and it's only your intention to perform logical fallacy games to play me as the fool in order to entertain your audience in the guise of a serious interview/discussion of ideas, in the manner in which your fellow RMN member Bill Hackett likes to perform—then

I will have to pass.
Very respectfully,
Malang Flathill

He got up to check on his family and tell Margaret about this new development when the charm rang notifying him of a new email.

Mr. Flathill,
You got it. No worries. You can promote whatever you like. Please let us know what date/time works best for you. I look forward to the interview!
Pat

Malang laughed aloud. What the heck was going on?

* * *

A week and a half later, Malang found himself in a black polo shirt sitting patiently in a quiet room on a live broadcast videoconferencing call, as Pat recited the episode's preamble. He listened carefully when the host began describing Malang's mission. "Our guest with us today is an interesting fellow. An artist and dedicated social justice warrior (yes, one of those) with a focus on policies that benefit 'ADOS,' the American Descendants of Slaves–which is what he's hoping the African-American community will start calling themselves now—to get Reparations. During the discussion, as always, we'll make time for questions from the live listening audience. Mr. Malang Flathill, how are you? I'm glad you could join us!"

"I'm very well, Pat. Thanks for having me. I'll admit I was surprised to receive your invite."

"What I would li—!" began Pat, but Malang quickly interrupted.

"Uh, before we get started let me make a quick correction to something you said in your intro." Pat started to reject the request, but then tossed his hands up in surrender.

"Go ahead. Sure."

"The name of the ADOS ethnic group is 'American Descendants of Slavery,' not 'slaves' as you accidentally put it. The accent is on slavery the institution; our wording of how we describe ourselves has to carefully put the emphasis on the specific identity group composed of the Black American former slave class. The way you said it would open the door for grifters to walk in. For example, scheming whites who had evidence their ancestors had been slaves somewhere on the globe could pull a fast one to get in on the ADOS Reparations program designed for the specificity our group needs to be made whole."

"Okay, that's… fine. We certainly want to make sure the right people get what's rightly due to them. I can't see how anyone would reasonably disagree with that. Since you've mentioned the term, I'd like to put 'identity politics' on the table now. As you may have heard, that's one of my pet bugbears, so to speak. For all of the Rational Murky Net, really. My question to you… may I call you 'Malang?' My question to you, Malang, is why do we need identity politics? Why can't we all just be Americans and work towards the healing of the nation as one group? Surely, you can agree that this divisive business is making society worse not better."

"Well, I don't have a problem with the concept of identity politics in the general sense," said Malang. "The way our government is designed is for a group of people with like interests to elect representatives to pressure the government to use its enormous spending power to provide what resources they require to thrive. No one can pretend that all Americans have the exact same interests throughout the nation. Some community interests are regional based, some are cultural based, etc. The better a community is at unifying and using the force of their political capital to get the government to move on their behalf, the more successful they will be long-term as a group. Of course, if the group is doing well, the less poverty the least members of the group will experience, in fact, they will have more opportunities to become successful. It turns out, all the major political decisions made in the last 400 years have been primarily beneficial to the dominant political identity group... the white Americans... who not coincidentally control 90% of the national household wealth. Those same major political decisions have been primarily detrimental to ADOS, who now live as the wealthless bottom caste group of the country. Getting us to that state involved sabotaging our political force, the force that worked so well during the civil rights era that it got major legislation passed. The sabotage of that force is why no major political legislation was passed on our behalf since then, and really, even those landmark acts were stripped of the force written into the original bills and turned into generic "all lives matter" laws that the already wealthy dominant political identity group could double-dip into. To answer your question, U.S. politics has always functioned on identity politics, but the modern rhetoric against it, from my point of view as an ADOS advocate for transformational politics for my people, appears to be designed to distract from the real activism in order to neutralize it."

"'My people,' you said. See, that's the kind of talk

I think we really need to get away from," said Pat.

"Why?"

"Why? Because they're not 'your' people. They're just 'people.'"

"They are the people," said Malang slowly. "with whom I share a specific lineage & heritage with—a shared historical narrative on a deeply personal level. When they are hurt, I'm hurt. When they are strong, then I am strong. The wrongs done to us we can't overcome lest we come together and overcome them as a group, and when we do, we can Never Forget Them lest they return during our ill-advised slumber. These are my people. The entire point of politics is to economically uplift the group! So, if I cannot identity the group to which I belong using specific labeling on a specific shared history, then how can I be lifted up? Also, what are the true motives of those trying to convince me that I don't need to identity my specific group, locking me out of access to the American benefits that such identification requires for American success?"

"I guess I just have a problem with this idea of living off the government's teat as a lifestyle." said Pat, wiping a sheen of sweat from a reddened face.

"You mean like the U.S. military personnel? Or any government employee, for that matter?"

"That's not the same…"

"Or what about all of the trillions and trillions of

dollars the U.S. government rained down upon the nation's white community and immigrants in the form of land grants, money and robust programs designed to create customized economic bubbles only whites enjoyed giving them this 90% control of the national household wealth head start? This was all made possible by white-controlled government and the insistence of their aligned white identity group constituency over generations. The whole time these same folk were locking ADOS out of access to these same wealth-building benefits they hoarded. The white community has for centuries enjoyed the benefits of skillfully, and often dishonestly, playing the game of identity politics in the political sphere—living off the gov's teat—and yet when ADOS rises with the fire of the civil rights movements of old, having recent presidential candidates publicly discussing Reparations for the first time in 80 years, somehow 'identity politics' has magically become a terrible, anti-American idea we have to get rid of immediately, right on cue." Malang glared into the camera with a sarcastic smirk.

"You think identity politics is a good thing, am I hearing you correctly?" asked Pat in a low tone.

"It's neither a good nor bad thing, Pat. It's a neutral tool used to access the resources of government in the way it was originally designed.

You're maybe not used to seeing it that way since the earliest Americans are described in limited ways in the educational indoctrination narratives, plus there were few of them. From my position I also see the early Americans from a particular way and stripped down to its literal and figurative 'black & white,' I recognize that identity politics has always been there. So much so, that for someone with the level of educational achievement you enjoy, it makes me suspicious as to why you are so against the idea of it now."

"Well, you're coming at it from a more generous angle as viewed through historical traditions. The modern left... and let me know your take on this... see it from a power-hungry agenda that's muddying the pot with all kinds of pseudo-science, would you agree?"

Malang sat up in his seat. "I think it's important to discern the difference between the normal identity group classification... so normal that people haven't really recognized it, or been made aware of it until this recent partisanization of the term... versus the left playing games with the concept and enabling white people to create identity group political classes so they can double-dip and be both of the wealthiest, most dominant group in the country, as well as pretend to be a protected minority group playing victim to their own oppression." Malang chuckled. Pat turned red again and seemed to be hesitant to pursue the topic further.

"Let's, uhh... you're an artist. So, you digitally paint your images and then sell them as prints, am I correct?"

"Yes, that's correct."

"And where can people find them?"

"Either on my blog or they can meet me at one of the local festivals in the Chocolate City vicinity."

"Are you formally trained, or...?"

"Yes, I have my BFA from an art school right here."

"Okay, that's good."

"I create from the same well of ideas that motivate my activism, from the anti-racism scholarship touching on systemic racism, et cetera, encouraging the political unification of my ADOS identity group so we can effectively organize to pressure our government for..."

"Oh, here's THAT buzz term. I knew it would come up eventually. 'Systemic racism.'"

"What about it?"

"You don't really believe in that, do you? I mean, how can we have 'systemic racism' when our systems comply to the laws that make it illegal to be racist! It's impossible," said Pat with an unmistakable smug tone in his voice.

"That sounds more like you have a laser focus on the individual meanings of the component words that make up the term, instead of taking time to understand what is actually meant by it. Assuming you'd care to know. If I tell you what it means, and you understand it, it'll make you 'woke.' Are you willing to risk that?" asked Malang with a chuckle. Pat started to retreat, his face till red, but then he tossed his hands.

"Okay, shoot. Let's hear it."

"U.S. systemic racism is the economic suppression of the group ADOS. Of course, racial discrimination is indeed illegal, but how do groups of Americans normally get around the law to work complex long-cons on the systemic level? It's called 'racketeering.' It's organized crime. That's certainly not impossible, it happens all the time and is extremely lucrative to particular groups of people who indulge in it as multi-generational lifestyle… all the way up to the top of the socioeconomic food chain where the 1% class sit. So, systemic racism is no less than unscrupulous white businessmen in partnership with unscrupulous white government officials at every level, using their power and networks to exploit and plunder ADOS so the former can get more at the expense of the latter. It's illegal, and it's been going on for the entire time I've been in this country."

"Don't forget that slavery was legal though," said Pat thoughtfully.

"Yes, and inside of that system there were numerous atrocities going on that were technically against even those immoral, unethical laws that the dominant classes were able to get away with because they were in agreement amongst one another as dedicated racketeers." Malang watched Pat as he reached offscreen. The sound of shuffling papers accompanied with Pat's irritated grunts made another smirk appear on Malang's face. Pat's already sweaty red face brightened when he glanced at the screen and he made a half-hearted, twitchy effort to compose himself.

"I just think we need to be careful in throwing all of these words around. Causing divisions and resentments… all it does is divide us."

"You think so? From my position, I'm curious as to what point in history when we weren't divided?" asked Malang.

"After the civil rights movement, we had…"

"We had what?"

"Uh, well, we had all of these programs…"

"Like affirmative action?"

"Exactly."

Malang shook his head. "When the 1964 Civil Rights and 1965 Voting Rights Acts were passed, the ADOS activist community led by Dr. Martin

Luther King, Jr. were actively working on a robust Reparations plan to provide a specific government program designed to pull ADOS out of the generational poverty centuries of accrued discrimination plunged us in. Then he was killed. The rest of that decade was a bloodbath as the most high-profile ADOS leaders were targeted and assassinated, one-by-one, and the top organizations infiltrated and dissolved. The surviving second and third tier leaders of the movement compromised, sold out and allowed our political rivals to dictate what they wanted the community to have instead of what we needed. So, instead of receiving the long-denied transformational specificity for our group, the gov provided "all lives matter" general programs for a generic "war on poverty" that whites could exploit. During the 19th and 20th centuries, whites received specificity GibsMeDats that ADOS were pointedly excluded from using the forced jim crow segregation laws that the white identity group voted for to hurt us and uplift themselves. When it came our turn to get uplifted so that we'd be economically competitive with whites, whites just gave themselves more gibs while creating 'welfare queen' narratives to funnel their anti-ADOS hatreds through."

"I'm, uhh… I'm going to take a call," said Pat, with an uncomfortable quiver in his voice. "Are you okay with that?"

"Sure, let's do it."

"Caller 6617? You're on the air."

"Hey, hi!" said a voice that sounded just like Pat. "Hello, fellas. My name's Derrick and frankly, I'm sick of listening to these... PEOPLE... blame everybody for their problems! I'm... I would like to know when are they ever going to take responsibility for what's going on in their own communities?!"

"Thanks, caller. That's fair. I think that's fair. Let's give our guest a chance to respond. Malang?"

"Okay, of course I recognize the classic partisan code for the 'black-on-black' crime trope. I'll answer it in two parts. For one, we are actually doing something about the desperate poverty-induced crime with numerous grassroots organizations and mentoring groups, some even in limited partnership with the local police departments. The problem with those is that they are limited without help from the government to address the root cause which is the trauma of artificially imposed impoverishment caused by that same complicit government. Which leads to the second point. Desperate crimes born from not having basic needs met is a mainstay of poor ADOS neighborhoods, but the modern urban warzone is a new development, a symptom of the so-called

'War on Drugs' campaign that turned out to be run by the Reagan administration's CIA. Its mission was to siphon the previous decade's wealth, built-up by the now extinct manufacturing jobs of the middle-class, to fund Reagan's sneaky, backdoor war machines. That was one part of it, but the other part was the radicalized hyper-violent gangs that trafficked the drugs and their addict victims became easy fodder for the rise of a new for-profit prison mass incarcerate state. This government-created mess that destroyed the ADOS communities and infested them with crime was done to us on purpose by the white people in government who had zero respect for our lives and only saw us as… well, the same way the slave holders of olde saw us… an exploitable thing that it was convenient to pretend wasn't really human anyway. Now folks like this Derrick act like the whole thing is our fault. We have many groups trying to control the evil after effects of what the most powerful government on earth deliberately did to us."

"Reparations," said Pat. He looked right into the camera.

It was difficult for Malang to interpret his tone. "Yes, a robust Reparations program designed to make us whole economically is how this can be fixed. This also involves economically including us into a protected wealth-building ownership class."

"You're not a slave though," said Pat.

"I literally just explained how the U.S. government just completely devastated our communities as one example of thousands of the ADOS community being exploited and plundered by the dominant identity group, but here you are still playing the 'Reparations is only for slavery' game. Reparatory Justice is due starting from the 1600s when the enslaved Africans were first permanently delegated to the bondsman class, through the sabotage and retraction of Reconstruction, a century of murderous 'strange fruit' domestic terror, decades of forced jim crow second class citizenship, political disenfranchisement and economic exclusion practices of even today, that are all the result of that anti-ADOS legacy. Reparations is for all of it. All."

"Okay, but who's going to pay for all of it?"

"What do you mean? Everybody who is not ADOS."

"Yeah, that's not going to fly..."

"It won't fly if we don't fight for it, that's for sure."

"I just don't see that happening," said Pat in a low mumble.

"Why not?" Malang raised his right eyebrow high. "I had to pay taxes for all kinds of programs which included reparations for internment camped Japanese Americans, for Holocaust victims, for Native Americans, etc., and I as a member of the

ADOS ethnicity certainly had nothing to do with any of those atrocities. There's an inherent cost that comes with wherever we live. This is true all over the world."

"Some of us are the sons and grandsons of immigrants. Why would we have to pay for Reparations?"

"That's why I mentioned the fact that I as an American citizen have to pay taxes for all kinds of reparations, no matter how controversial they were at the time, for atrocities that I had even less to do with, since the World Wars, for example, were mostly white-on-white crimes. Do we ever get to choose which programs we get to pay taxes on? Then why this unusual speak whenever Reparations for the group that made all of these wonderful American Dream opportunities available for everyone else to enjoy?"

"Alright. Well, I don't know if we can wring anything else out of that topic. Let's move on."

"Okay." Malang took a sip of the tea Margaret handed him out of camera range.

"What about this 'third eye' thing. I'll admit that I was trying to keep an open mind while I was reading your accounts, but I…" Pat shook his head looking at his notes. "Basically, I don't know where to put it."

Malang laughed along with his host. "Well,

they were real experiences that happened to me. I felt the best thing I could do, outside of my responsibility to meditate upon what was shown to me in the visions, was to describe it in as much detail as I could and make it available so that others could possibly recognize the experiences that they had that matched. In my highest optimism, I imagined that eventually a bunch of people who had the same experience would come together and we'd build a database capable of being studied for posterity."

"That's all?" asked Pat with a raised eyebrow.

"That's all."

"I just thought that, combined with your argumentative lectures and preaching, that it was intended to elevate you to some kind of spiritual figure."

"No. I reject any of that stuff. The only figures who were worthy of that role were the prophets of olde, and that age is definitively over per the Word of the One God."

"And what 'word' would that be?"

"The Qur'an," said Malang with firmness.

"Ah. So, you are Muslim?"

"Yes."

"Okay, that's interesting. And you are advocating for the political empowerment and pro-reparations, etc., for the African-Americans. For

ADOS."

"I am an ADOS Muslim."

"I wonder what Louis Farrakhan thinks about all of this?"

"I'm an orthodox Muslim, Pat, following the Qur'an and way of the unlettered Ishmaelite prophet Muhammad (*peace be upon him*). I've never had any affiliation with the Nation of Islam in any of its forms. As far as I know, as a Caribbean-American in his own lineage, Farrakhan is pro-Pan-Africanist, pro-Black immigrant in his political leanings and may or may not support the specificity agenda of the ADOS Reparations program. The ADOS Advocacy Foundation does have a Black Political Agenda that includes the Black immigrants though, but that is very strictly separate from the Reparations portion which is for the American Descendants of Slavery ethnic group alone."

"Let me take a call. Hey, caller 2121, you're on the air."

"Yeah, thank you for taking my call. Uhhh, As-Salaam Alaikum, Brother Malang! Where in the Holy Qur'an does Allah talk about the 'third eye,' brother? My name is Brother Shabazz by the way. Not trying to be rude, but can you answer my question, brother?"

"Wa Alaikum As-Salaam," responded Malang,

returning the traditional Abrahamic greeting in the Arabic language as is the Islamic custom. "It does not. The One God does not talk about the specific 'third eye' phenomenon. What is mentioned often is that the One God is the Author of the signs that point to His Majesty and Glory. The 'third eye' event is most definitely a sign of God; by no means do I partner with the pagans in assigning it any kind of meaning outside of what the One God revealed about humanity's glimpses into the unseen spirit. I was blessed with personal inspiration to guide me in my walk on the Straight Way and nothing more. I make no claims to being another prophet of God, a spiritual guru, a magical teacher or anything else I have no authority to claim. All I can attest is that the three events really did happen to me and I share the experiences to add to the body of human knowledge. That's all."

"That's well and good and everything, brother, but how do you know this wasn't the shaitan whispering to you, brother?"

"All I know is what I described in the blog. There was nothing trying to influence me into something wrong or anything like that. All three 'third eye' openings were only positive experiences, the fruit of which, was the strengthening of my faith in the Most-High."

"Well, it seems to me, brother, that this 'ADOS'

group you've hooked up with is the negative whispering influence since everything I've heard about them is negative, brother! They're just divisive and splitting up the community!"

Malang narrowed his eyes as he looked into the camera. "As ADOS, a member of the Black American former slave class…"

"We're only slaves to Allah, brother!!"

"Of course," Malang smiled patiently. "I'm saying that as a member of that particular ethnic group, my heritage is one in which I am descended from a controlled group, legally enslaved according to the laws of the land for 230 years. The exploitation of my group amassed the obscene wealth of the West and it made my enemies greedy to the point of cultivating a multi-generational legacy of obsession to keep my people subjugated for continued exploitation for their benefit. Numerous groups joined in this demonic feeding frenzy, which included the Black immigrant groups. After 60 yrs of grifting my community, the only identified fruit of 'Pan-Africanism' and it's 'flat blackness' ideology, is the political disenfranchisement of my people and the elevation of all other Black ethnicities who apparently came to use my people as mules. It's time for my group to wake up from that treachery and unify along our own unique lineage and heritage to pressure our government for our own economic uplift."

"You don't need to be following those two ADOS founders, brother! They not even Muslims, for one! And they obviously leading you astray, brother!"

"In my experience, the two founders of the #ADOS movement—attorney Antonio Moore and former Democratic Party aid Yvette Carnell—have only been on the up-and-up… using a relentless data-driven approach to their politico-economic analysis that is thus far unparalleled among those claiming to be leaders of the ADOS community. They have used their commentary and guidance to advocate for organizing to achieve our long-withheld Reparatory Justice and economic inclusion into a protected wealth-building ownership class, with an energy we haven't seen since the who's who of civil rights leaders still walked among us. They are rightly-guided. Our job is to bring our A-Game to join them, and for those who believe that means a very specific thing. The Black American Muslim needs to join the ADOS Advocacy Foundation to use your talents and skills to get our ethnic group where we need to be in this country we've built."

"Alright. That's all I got, brother. As-Salaam Alaikum."

"Wa Alaikum As-Salaam."

Pat cleared his throat, a look on his face as if he

had witnessed a private family dispute. "That was awkward, huh?"

"No, not really. I anticipated some pushback from some believers. The divide & conquer tactics of my ideological foe are multi-tentacled after-all. There's more than one way to disenfranchise a people and, with trillions and trillions of hoarded wealth at stake, why wouldn't my enemy use all of them?"

"So, the essence of your discussion with the caller," said Pat. "is that you believe your Islamic faith is compatible with this social justice ADOS activism?"

"Yes. As long as the ADOS Muslim follows the tenets of his/her religion, there is no conflict there."

"What are those tenets?"

"Believe in the One God who made you, perform righteous deeds, reject wrongdoing, repent when you mess up and be not obstinate in doing wrong. For the ADOS believer to 'strive with might & main in the cause of the One God' is to work right in their backyard, awakening the dormant political might of their own ethnic group to pull us out of the wealthless bottom caste. As I mentioned in my blog, I rationalized that idea out and started following it. When I started doubting the logic of it myself, that's when I had my first 'third eye' opening and I recognized it as no less than a spiritual sign of encouragement, letting me know I was on the right course. It's important for believers to be able to discern truth from falsehood, the signs of the One God from paganism. Having rational discussions to talk about it like adults is important."

"You're using rational and 'third eye' in the same sentence. That's funny."

"Pat, did you read in my blog posts where I explained that I had studied the 'third eye' lore and knew the background of it. That's why I knew what the phenomenon was as it was happening to me. It's a concept and personal experience that has been studied by the ancients for millennia and there is a rational thread to be studied for people who care about the material. It sounds like you have never studied it and yet have a bias against the material based on some negative connotations, similar to what Brother Shabazz just said a minute ago. I 100% understand since I also had a similar dismissive attitude about that stuff before I actually looked into it. I think you should stand-down until you have a base of knowledge to argue from, instead of just assuming it's a fiction because you believe it is from a biased and uninformed position, 'Doctor.'"

Pat laughed. "Okay, yes, I do see your logic and rationale and I can agree to a certain extent, but come on."

"You want me to ignore the study I've done on it, ignore my experiences, to instead partner with you in dismissing it because you prefer to dismiss it."

"You're putting words in my mouth, Malang."

"Then how else am I supposed to interpret your 'but come on?'" Pat sat silent for a tense few moments as he thought about the question. "Doesn't 'but come on' mean that you want me to stop thinking what I think and start thinking like you think, Pat? It implies that I'm not serious, right?"

"You are serious is what you're saying."

"Yes, Pat."

"How do you know it's what you think it is?"

"Because I was fortunate to have studied the material, read the accounts of people over the ages who had the experience and described it the best way they could to compare my experiences with. This includes the over-poetic language of Ancient Egyptian descriptions, as well as Dr. Hessians' account as I referenced in the blog posts. That's why I think it's valuable for there to be a formal body of literature composed of the submitted accounts of people who have any kind of paranormal experience. If we have the compiled data, we can develop effective methods to study it, methods that are currently missing since Western Civilization doesn't hold value in those subjects currently."

"I can appreciate your faith in these things, in the material as you say. I just don't think this kind of magical thinking has done society any good. Some of the worst atrocities in history have taken place in the name of religions."

"Give me an example, please," Malang asked.

"Seriously? There are thousands, at least."

"Give me the classic example of what you're talking about then, please."

"Alright. The crusades." Pat flipped his hands up and sat them back on his desk. "Look at all the deaths that came from those religious wars."

"The root cause of the crusades conflict, was the fact that the monarchs of Europe saw that non-Christians had taken control of the Abrahamic holy lands and, far from religious piety motivations, saw the opportunity to conquer the region for self-serving reasons. This was not a 'religious' conflict, but a typical warmongering monarchical conflict of the usual sort. The fact that the crusaders were infamous thugs who killed fellow Christians they encountered along the way and confiscated their stuff, too, was evidence that the conflict had nothing to do with the religion they pretended to subscribe to."

"I guess what I'm looking for," offered Pat. "is what the link is between your 'third eye' thing and your ADOS activism."

"There isn't one. Not as far as the public is concerned. It's important to me, as I said, because it's a personal experience. How I interpret it and use it to guide my faith walk doesn't have anything to do with anyone else. My job is to study scripture and aim to be the best Muslim I can be."

"You think being a good Muslim is to be a political activist."

"Absolutely. I'm sure you've seen all of the leftist memes pointing out that the Christ Jesus (*peace be upon him*) functioned as a political radical in how the messenger is described in the New Testament, so the concept is not alien to you. Being religious in the Abrahamic tradition has never represented sitting on a mountain somewhere and not being engaged in community. Look at the Black church tradition in how it led the fight during both abolition and the civil rights era. For me as an ADOS Muslim, in the nation where my people are artificially impoverished into a wealthless bottom caste, the advocacy for organization and the fight for transformational politics to make my people whole after all these centuries of abuse is the ultimate worthy cause. Important indeed within a religion that is all about believing in the One God and performing righteous deeds as evidence of that belief. It will be a win/win on both the earthly side and the spiritual side in the proverbial 'two birds with one stone' stroke. To return to the other point, you'll find that few of your 'religious atrocities' are actually religious in nature and are in fact classic, secular, greed-fueled conflicts. Rarely are people being actually attacked because they aren't following the attacker's religion. What we have going on today, is the United States empire managing itself on behalf of megacorporate. That partnership involves the latter needing the resources of foreign lands for industry and instead of negotiating peacefully with sovereign governments to pay market prices for goods, they instead have the CIA write up phony 'WMD' reports as an excuse to have the U.S. military come in and bust heads so megacorporate can snatch up the resources for free."

"Yeah, well, you're not really saying anything we don't already know on that score…"

"You say that and yet that doesn't keep you from parroting the same 'religious atrocity' rhetoric absent from insight into the corporate/government imperialist empire building that's really the primary source of the world's atrocities."

Pat let out a huge sigh. "Alright, this is… this has been one exhausting interview for me. Can't say I really enjoyed it. Did you, uh, have anything else you wanted to say or whatever before we wrap up?"

"Oh! Yes, for any Black Americans of the former

slave class who may be listening in," said Malang, sitting up and pulling his chair closer to the monitor. "The reason why you are hearing anything negative about the #ADOS movement, seeing all of these poorly researched and slanderous hit piece articles out there about the group, is because it really is the real thing. There are negative propaganda attacks against the movement because we are picking up the baton dropped by a tragically slain Dr. Martin Luther King, Jr. and likewise 'coming to get our check.' The bad guys of the story felt that it was worth murdering Dr. King and his fellow uncompromising pro-Black American leaders in order to maintain their gross monopoly over the nation's power structures and resources, so obviously it should go without saying that they would have zero qualms about slandering an authentic, grassroots political advocacy group who is all about the same mission and not the lifestyle of individual members living like wannabe priest-kings at the top, like all the other 'black organizations' that have let us down along the way. We can finally win this thing if we leverage our dormant political might by organizing under #ADOSAF leadership so that we can effectively pressure our government for the Reparations and economic inclusion we are owed. Do not listen to anybody else, even those skinfolk wearing our face, if they claim otherwise. Please visit the adosfoundation.org website and checkout the content of Antonio Moore's tonetalks and Yvette Carnell's BreakingBrown channels to get caught up. Thank you for listening. Peace."

* * *

Agent Phillip Konde sat at a dark corner booth in an inconspicuous Chocolate City diner staring at his phone at close to shock. Malang did Pat Wertheim the same way he did him, Konde thought. He not only held his own against the infamous RMN member, but he ran right over him; Pat didn't know what to do with Malang's calm, history-backed responses. Like Konde, he also took for granted that most people respond in a canned partisan template that's easy for talented, sharp men like Wertheim and him to spin.

So, who is this Malang really? Despite his claims to not be some kind of mystical guru, Konde was no longer sure. He went to Malang's blog and carefully reread the 'third eye' posts with a different frame of mind than before, this time with a wary open-mindedness that Malang maybe wasn't just a kook. By the time he made the fifth pass on the third blog post, Special Agent Konde had quietly decided he would be a follower of Malang Flathill and, even though he himself was not ADOS, he would use his Federal Government-trained skills to aid him in his pro-#ADOS movement stance. Gesturing towards a waitress, he paid his bill and stepped out into the city.

* * *

"What in the hell was THAT?!?" shouted Director Raye. Pat prudently pulled the cell phone away from his ear. "Your dumbass was supposed to humiliate this blackie, not give him free airtime to spew that social justice shit all over the damned world!!" Pat wasted 30 minutes trying to calm the F.B.I. director down, who seemed to only get even more irate with the attempt. His overconfidence in deciding to do the show live was his undoing; how was he supposed to know this Malang guy was a real activist and sharp as a tack? Or the guy at least knew how to talk the talk like one and Pat couldn't say he ever really had experience dealing with that crowd. He only thought he did. What did Malang say? That most of those SJWs were just scammers taking advantage of the Civil Rights Act to double-dip? Pat may not have been willing to buy the conspiracy against ADOS thing (at least not the whole thing), but the other part seemed to be legit based on the cancel-culture experience of the Rational Murky Net themselves against these clowns.

"Do you understand me?!?" Oops. Pat had tuned the director out. He'll try to bluff him.

"Yes, sir. As I said, I do apologize for…"

"SHOVE YOUR APOLOGY UP YOUR ASS!!!"

Wow. This is our Federal Government, ladies and gentlemen, thought Pat. He briefly considered the possible consequences for hanging up on the F.B.I.

Nah. As far as Pat knew, it was the F.B.I. who sicced those other SJWs on him just to put him in this damned position.

"Is there something… what can I do to make this up?"

"JACK SHIT!!!" To Pat's relief, the director hung up on him.

* * *

Shaking with fury, Director Raye poured two-fingers of his brownish-gold liquor into his glass. He started to put the cap on the bottle, but tossed the cap aside and set the bottle on the table with a thump. He wanted to feel regretful for putting Pat on the assignment, but there was no indication he would fail so spectacularly. Raye was forced to admit he didn't know the strengths and capabilities of each RMN member as well as he thought. The phone rang and he felt a headache-inducing tension when he saw the caller ID display a row of pound symbols instead of the incoming number.

"Yes, your Grey Eminences."

"Your failure is awesome to behold. Awesome indeed," said a low-toned, gruff voice. "When you fail in your duties, it comes back on us. This is unacceptable."

"I understand, I'll just…" Raye stammered.

"Do you understand?" asked this representative of The Grey Eminences. "If you understood, you wouldn't have failed."

"I'll take care of it."

"What you'll do is jot down these two numbers, contact the parties on the other side, and have them handle this annoying blackie. Are you holding a pen?"

"I… Y-yes. YES! I got it." The Grey Eminence dictated the phone numbers and hung up. Director Raye used the resources at his disposal to find out who sat on the other side of the two numbers before he called. One was a satellite affiliate of the RMN, their ally, one who refused to be publicly considered an actual member even though all of his beliefs aligned perfectly with theirs. The other name belonged to a high-profile former Muslim turned Christian convert. Director Raye snatched up the phone to call them right away. At least if they failed, it wouldn't be on him! Whether the hidden hand would see it that way… well, he'd find out soon enough one way or another.

6

Unleash the Patty-Rollers

Malang allowed the computer-sounding female voice of the GPS direct him towards the television station in Ferntop, a suburban city laying adjacent to Chocolate City's North West side.

After his Black Sheep Podcast interview a couple of weeks ago, the Flathill family enjoyed the thrill of a viral promotion, with several offers to do more interviews coming in. The GPS voice instructed Malang to turn his burgundy sedan to the right at a side street with yet another falafel deli sitting on the corner, a hallmark of Ferntop's large Middle-Eastern immigrant community. Malang chose to take this particular interview on the *Ferntop's Speaks!* show as it would be his first television appearance and he thought it would be fun. The host, Umar Hammoud, wasn't exactly a household name since the show was local, but it had featured appearances with Arab and/or Muslim celebrity guests over the years, which included both active and retired appearances by the late boxer Muhammad Ali.

The GPS announced that Malang had arrived at his destination and he got busy finding a parking spot that wasn't hiding a ticket trap of some kind — a tricky affair that took over 20 minutes to solve — but fortunately he'd built just such a situation into his travel time.

The building was a single-story tan brick with white trim. Malang entered and adjusted the navy-blue blazer he decided to wear over his signature light gray, long-sleeved t-shirt. Margaret side-eyed him when he put it on, so he added his brown dress shoes to receive her quiet click of semi-approval. The receptionist welcomed him to sit until the crew was ready for him and Malang could hear the host chatting it up with whoever his co-guests were from the receptionist's monitor. Malang thought to recognize one of the guest's voices, and spent a futile few moments trying to place it. Nothing in the content of their banter was providing a clue since, whatever the original nature of their discussion had been, it had now devolved into a silly fluff in the wind down. Malang noticed a quick movement from the receptionist, who then got up to direct him towards the awaiting action.

The stage area was composed of a backdrop of a *Ferntop Speaks!* graphics imagery — a black & white photo collage of guests from throughout the decades — behind a foot-high raised platform on which sat four chairs. A camera crew of up to 6-7 people milled about outside of the lighted stage area, and to Malang's surprise, there was no studio audience seating, which popped the bubble of his expectations. Umar Hammoud welcomed him warmly with practiced ease and introduced him to the other two guests: Jerome Bazzi, a former Muslim turned Christian convert and Professor Joe Arazi, he of the familiar voice Malang had recognized.

"Brother Malang, you are one of the leaders of this ADOS movement, yes?" asked Umar. Malang shook his head.

"No, sir. I'm a member of the American Descendants of Slavery ethnic group to whom the movement's non-profit organization—ADOS Advocacy Foundation—organizes on behalf. As an 'art activist,' it is my duty to support them and spread awareness of their mission so that as many ADOS as possible get to have the opportunity to join in the effort to achieve our political goals. Those goals are 1.) Reparations for ADOS, 2.) the economic inclusion into a protected wealth-building ownership class for ADOS, and 3.) the Black Political Agenda for the greater community of Black Americans which includes ADOS."

Umar nodded with a serious look on his face. "Very good. I see."

"I listened to your interview with my friend Pat Wertheim," said Professor Arazi. "I wouldn't have easily guessed you were a Muslim until you said so. Why do you prefer the use of the English 'One God' over the Arabic 'Allah?' I'm curious."

"That's because I am a native-born American citizen with English as my mother tongue. I know the Islamic tradition is to use the Arabic terms all the time, but I see no reason to adhere to that custom as if it is a condition of the faith itself. Note that the usage of the Arabic language isn't in the Five Pillars of Islam, no more than usage of the Hebrew is one of the Ten Commandments." This elicited a murmur of outrage among the three.

"Astaghfirullah, brother!!" shouted Umar with a red face. "The Arabic language is holy as it is the language of the Holy Qur'an itself! Allah called the language the perspicuous tongue! How can you say these things?"

"I do not doubt it is perspicuous as God confirmed, which is a concept most relevant to you, O People of the Book who received it from the anointed messenger (*peace be upon him*) who preached it directly to you in your own tongue. It was your responsibility to study it, understand it and get it to the non-Arabic speaking globe. That's why it came to you in your own tongue, using descriptions and metaphors of special meaning to your local community. It's not my job to convert to Arabism, Ishmaelite-ism, or even Hejaz-ism to become a Muslim. Translating the Word of the One God into my native tongue so that I can understand it and have the opportunity to know the message of my Lord is your job as a People of the Book."

"Brother," said Jerome cautiously. "The term 'People of the Book' is understood to refer to Christians and Jews."

"In the Qur'an," said Malang. "the One God uses the term to refer to both of those two groups together and separately based on the context of the given verses. It means, in context, a people to whom a Book was revealed that they are charged to guard and champion. Isn't the Saudi government calling itself the 'guardians of the two sacred mosques?' Likewise, the Arab community are the guardians of the Qur'an. Being a 'People of the Book' comes with a great blessing and prestige, but also a great responsibility. If you lot had continued the unfortunate centuries-old tradition of refusing to translate the Qur'an, unreasonably making everyone jump through the hoop of converting to Arabism to know the message of the One God, then it would have been my duty to do your job for you and find a way to get it translated for my people."

An uncomfortable tense silence settled over the group. Malang adjusted himself in his chair, barely managing to suppress a smirk. Professor Arazi watched Malang warily, his fingers forming a tent in front of him as the color in his cheeks deepened.

"I get the impression that you, a self-identified descendant of American Black slaves," said Professor Arazi in a low growl. "are somehow projecting that you are a better Muslim than the Arabs? That you are better capable of interpreting Al-Qur'anu than the native Arabic speaker? Obviously, any English translation would be inferior to the pure Arabic Qur'an."

"I'm not claiming to be a better Muslim for no other reason than because of my lineage and heritage, no. That type of foolish mistake has been done in the earth quite enough." Malang noticed the professor's eyes flash and he looked away. "I'm only saying that there is no inherent virtue in learning the Arabic language, and as long as you have done your duty and translated it properly, the English version is just fine for my purposes."

"Astaghfirullah!" cried Umar for the second time. Malang chuckled and focused his attention upon his host.

"Okay, answer me this, Umar: Did not the One God say that He raised up a prophet among EVERY people – some He told us about in the Book, most He did not? Do you remember?"

"Well, yes," admitted Umar hesitantly.

"That means that since Adam the patriarch (*peace be upon the first prophet*) the Word of the One God was revealed through all of humankind's languages. All. Do you understand? So, if Arabic is magically holy because the Qur'an was revealed wrapped within that linguistic packaging, then they are ALL holy for the same reason. Just because past unenlightened peoples failed to preserve their precious charges like the Qur'an was so preserved doesn't matter – the countless previous versions of the Book still came down in the words of those countless local prophets' tongues."

"The English language had no prophet, brother," said Umar.

"Don't be so sure. The earliest versions of English are tracked to at least the 5th century, which is older than the prophet Muhammad's mission (*peace be upon him*). How do you know that an unknown prophet hadn't been anointed among those unknown peoples? We cannot know this, but we can take what the One God said as true on faith though, and recognize that there was indeed a window of time in which there very well could have been an Old English-speaking prophet of the One God."

Another annoyed murmur circulated among the three. Jerome leaned in to whisper something to Professor Arazi who smiled and looked up at Malang.

"Brother Malang, are you trying to imply that you are an English prophet of Allah?"

"By no means!" said Malang with force. "I would

never say what I had no right to say! I bear witness that there is no god but the One God and the unlettered Ishmaelite prophet Muhammad was His final messenger—with all that may imply. I am only a believing servant of God and no more. My job is to study scripture so I know what my Lord requires of me and pass it along to aid those with an ear to hear the One God's message."

"Then why do you challenge the authority of the people whose native language is Arabic and know the Qur'an best?"

Malang looked puzzled. "I recognize it is a great honor to have had a prophet raised up among you and to be a People of the Book, but I see no evidence of an 'authority' over me because of this. Curious of you to say that. In the Qur'an, the One God said that He made us different that we may learn from one another and He also said that we are to 'compete with each other in righteousness.' The Divine challenge is obvious. We are to learn the translated scripture in our own tongues, master it within our own local managed affairs and compete with one another to see who does it best. No harm can come from such a 'Contest of the Believing Righteous' – in truth, it could only make the earth a better place. In addition to the Ultimate Reward of paradise, there is nothing I want more than for my people, the ADOS ethnic group, to seize the Word of the One God with an unbreakable double-fisted grip and master it, besting you all as the demonstrated best Muslims in the world in the Sight of their Guardian Lord! This is my personal challenge to my own identity group, to use our legendary 'Black Excellence' to great effect and leave the rest of you – even you, O arrogant Arab! – to eat our dust!"

The three laughed, followed by another murmur among them with a more relaxed, albeit patronizingly dismissive, good humor. Umar started to speak, but Jerome raised his hand towards Malang signaling for his attention.

"Brother, it is my understanding that your ADOS are traditionally a Christian group. Do you not feel a longing to return to the pure message of your Lord and Savior Jesus Christ?"

"That is the dominant religious tradition of my people true, but my personal experience is that I was born to a couple who had converted to Islam before I arrived. I have no 'Christian tradition' within my own experiences." Jerome pouted in unmistakable disappointment. As he struggled to recover, Professor Arazi leaned forward.

"Ah," he said. "So, that is why you are a Muslim. Because you were raised in a Muslim household then. Were you raised in a Christian household, then it would be Christianity you'd be extolling!"

Triumphantly, Professor Arazi leaned back into his seat.

"The fact that both of my parents were raised Christians would appear to shootdown your epiphany, Professor. I made the conscious decision to commit to the religion when I was in my early 20s. Before that, I cannot say I held any solid anchor in the faith outside of a child's longing for his parent's approval. Please note all of the baby boomer white people who seemed to almost *en masse* abandon their Christian and even Jewish family creeds to go running pell-mell after Far Eastern traditions and mysticisms trying to be the next Alan Watts or Robert Anton Wilson or whomever."

Another tense silence from the group, with Professor Arazi glaring at Malang with an emotion he couldn't quite assess. Was he angry? Malang wondered if his presence here wasn't coincidental; that he had actually come to have a go at Malang himself after he felt his RMN buddy was disrespected? Malang decided to interpret the professor's comments through that lens moving forward and see how the rest of the discussion would go. He sat up in his seat.

"I know that some of what I said here has perhaps ruffled some of you all's Islamic-flavored, national identity sensibilities," Malang volunteered. "but

I don't think it's a good thing to strut about in the land arrogantly, acting like you are superior in Islam just because you are a People of the Book. The One God pointedly told us as believers to compete in righteousness, which obviously comes with effort, work ethic. Pretending you are magically better Muslims because the prophet was raised up among your ancestors and you came into this world with the Qur'an on your parent's bookshelf is how you build a lazy entitlement into your religious expression that will only create more unbelieving 'cultural Muslims.' Acting like you have a privileged faux-monopoly over God and His religion is how the children of Israel act, and no good comes from that attitude. Stop trying to force your language upon other peoples; it's wrong. The message of the One God is universal. Call to mind when God warned both Semite nations that He could destroy you and raise up a new people who would follow the message in righteous devotion and full submission to their Guardian Lord. This is my charge to my ADOS group here! We ARE that 'New People!' If God be on our side we cannot lose in our fight for Reparations! Let's use the political guidance of the ADOS Advocacy Foundation IN THE NAME OF GOD that we may prosper!"

"Brother, the real God is Jesus Christ who calls you forth with the love of a father, not a demand for the submission of a slave!" said Jerome, raising his voice to keep from being cut off again.

"Fatherhood is a concept the One God created for the procreating creatures of His creation, it has nothing to do with Him. God is God, He is not a 'father.' Remember the account of Abraham (*peace be upon him*) and the sonship sacrifice? The One God waited almost a century to gift the prophet He called His friend a son and then told him to sacrifice the boy. The worship the One God demands is unhesitant, complete submission to the Divine Will. The ill-advised father analogy was developed by men to bring the Majesty of the Most-High down to a lower level they can better manage within narrow minds. God is not your father, He is God."

"I do not recognize your god," said Jerome defiantly.

"There is only One God," Malang responded. "God told you who He was and what type of worship He requires of us in the book you hold. Will you substitute God's unambiguous requirements for your own father-cult invention for no other reason than your unreasonable, sinful preference for paganism? Have a care."

"All I know," said Jerome with tearful passion. "is that Islam never spoke to me! Only the living waters of the Word of the Christian faith spoke to me and called me to salvation!"

Malang watched as Umar clumsily handed Jerome a box of tissues to clean his face.

"See, one of the weaknesses that come with being a People of the Book, is the temptation to take the faith for granted as a part of your national identity background. A similitude is when people who live in a particular city take for granted that they know their city. Usually, tourists will know the special sites and landmarks better than the natives because they actually took the time to study it and visit all the special places, while the natives just live their mundane lives ignoring the specialness of their city as a barely noticed backdrop. The 'cultural Muslim' has failed to become a 'tourist' to learn your 'city' with fresh eyes, and thus doomed yourself as a transgressor of faith."

Jerome bristled. "What?! Do you as an American Muslim dare suggest that my expression of Islam was inferior when you don't even speak Arabic?!"

"It is written in verse 17:39," said Malang. "'Take not, with Allah, another object of worship, lest thou shouldst be thrown into Hell, blameworthy and rejected.'"

"How dare you!" shouted Jerome, his eyes shining with anger. "You're not going to recite at me…!'

"It is written in verse 3:85," said Malang, cutting him off. "'If anyone desires a religion other than

Islam, submission to Allah, never will it be accepted of him; and in the Hereafter He will be in the ranks of those who have lost all spiritual good!'"

"I drink from the cup of living water! I reject…!" Spittle flying from Jerome's lips as he tried to take command of the discussion.

"It is written in verse 3:90," said Malang. "'But those who reject Faith after they accepted it, and then go on adding to their defiance of Faith, never will their repentance be accepted, for they are those who have of set purpose gone astray!' Jerome, will you abandon the religion God said He perfected for you—without having actually studied it!—to worship the final Hebrew prophet in the line of Isaac (*peace be upon him*) and think you won't suffer the irresistible Wrath of the One who made you? You don't have an argument here, Jerome, and you certainly hold nothing that I would be willing to risk eternal torment for. I suggest you repent and bow down to the One who made you alone."

"Uhhh, brothers, let us please not turn this into a fight. That is not why we are here," said Umar with his arms raised. "Maintain a peaceful environment. Please."

In a quiet tone, Jerome addressed Malang holding the handful of tissues tight. "Jesus said that no one will get to the father except through him."

"He was correct," Malang responded. "At the time

he said it, the Christ was the only anointed prophet-messenger of God on earth, the living Word. This is the role that all the prophet-messengers were in—from Adam the patriarch to the unlettered Ishmaelite Muhammad—and they all performed their duties most excellently confirmed by the Lord thy God Himself. Glory be to He!"

"My savior would never have his children slaving away performing works that will never be enough to earn his love! The blood and grace of the father will suffice for my salvation," said Jerome.

"Not so. That is not how God's religion works. Call to mind Luke 18:18-25, where the rich, young ruler approached the Christ and point blank asked him what he needed to do in order to be saved. Did the Christ start reciting that 'blood and grace of the father' business with him? No. The anointed master of scripture told him to first keep the Commandments, which are of course composed of the 'Thou Shalt Not...!' rules – meaning avoid wrongdoing. Next, he was told to spend all of his wealth. That is to say, for someone who has spent his life hoarding the riches of this illusory world and eschewing the promise of the unseen spirit, he needed to spend out of the bounty God provided in God's cause – perform righteous deeds. In other words, the instructions as to how one who believes can become saved as instructed by the

Christ himself in your own book, is by avoiding wrong doing and doing good deeds, exactly what the religion you abandoned said to do from the pure revealed message, so how is it you are deluded away from the truth?"

Malang noticed that Professor Arazi's eyes were comically wide as he stared at him. He knew they couldn't have too much more time to go and he was growing impatient that the professor hadn't yet made his move. Perhaps Malang was simple wrong about him deliberately coming here to out-argue Malang on behalf of his buddy?

"Professor, I'm curious as to how the Arab community can match the Jewish community in your adoration for the concept of patriarchal-nationhood," said Malang, hoping to bait the professor into a lively scuffle. He realized he had never really dug into what Arazi's actual pet rants were, outside of the general RMN platform. "Didn't you study the nature of the Christ's great miracle?"

"What is Jesus' great miracle?" asked Jerome. Malang glanced at him.

"That he was conceived without the seed of an earthly father," said Malang, returning his gaze to lock onto Professor Arazi's eyes. "This cut him off from his patriarchal line, which was all important to the children of Israel who built their entire identity around the concept. Since their brethren nation hold similar views, I wanted to know what Professor Arazi's take on it was from the position of the Arab."

"I'm not an Arab," said the professor dryly.

"What?" Malang was genuinely taken aback. Professor Arazi's facial features—a shiny, deeply-tanned Caucasian skin tone of the over-affluent, a large nose with an unmistakable hook-like shape, dark eyes with eyelashes thick enough to seem like they were enhanced with mascara—he assumed that he was of Middle Eastern descent. "Wh-where are your people from?"

"Lebanon," said Arazi and Umar in unison.

"From Lebanon? But you're not...?"

"I'm Jewish."

"Oh," Malang said, sitting back in his seat. "Sorry, I didn't know. I'll withdraw the question."

"No, no, it's fine. It just means you didn't read my book." The group laughed. "I'll sign a copy for you."

"Would you be willing to take a stab at the question, Umar?" asked Malang of their host who immediately blushed.

"Uhh... What was the question again?"

"How do you regard the Christ's great miracle of being a prophet with no patriarchal-national lineage tie, a concept that we all know is very important to the two Semite nations? What do you think of that clear message from the One God to the two of you?"

Umar stumbled over himself a bit, hemmed & hawed while his two clearly uncomfortable guests looked away. They darted angry glances at Malang who released Umar from the spell with a welcome shift in gears. "To me, it forces you – us – to focus in on the Christ's actual messaging and not the incidentals that we humans use to manage our affairs with. God doesn't care about those (nationality, race, gender, etc.), just whether our deliberate behaviors are aligned to His commands."

"And what exactly is the Christ's actual messaging?" asked Jerome with a hint of sarcasm.

"What he instructed the rich, young ruler," snapped Malang. "Are we going to revisit that now after you've already cowered from the lesson?" Jerome angrily sat back in his seat. Malang successfully resisted the immature urge to roll his eyes.

"So, this artwork that you do," said Umar, dabbing at the sweat on his brow. "is it religious or for this political activism, or…?"

"Right now, it's primarily to support the #ADOS movement, but there are some spillover pieces when I feel the spiritual message is relevant." Malang turned his attention back to Professor

Arazi, who seemed as if he had lost interest in the entire affair. "Professor, you mentioned that you were 'Jewish.' I noted the use of the term. Does that mean you are nonpracticing and only identify with the religion from a proud cultural identity position, like Brother Jerome here does for Islam?"

"Yes. I am an atheist," said the professor with barely a glance. "I prefer the comforting warmth of science, logic and common sense over this lunatic demonstration of emotional fits screaming dusty old book quotes at each other."

Malang grinned and Umar started to hold up his hands. "The books are old, granted… the revealed message to humankind is as old as the species itself, so sayeth the Lord. Being old is not an inherent problem. The message was sent down specifically to guide the human being of earth to right conduct. For as long as we remain human it will continue to be ever relevant."

"Quite," said Professor Arazi dismissively. "It's clear at this point that you do know your stuff as far as your commitment to the religion is concerned. I'll admit I haven't studied it as in depth as you have, nor am I motivated to do so. I would like to return to this social justice warrior track you are on, foolishly adding to the death of the West by supporting this new culture of never-ending offense and victimhood."

"I advocate for the end of systemic racist oppression of my ethnic group, Professor. Those offenses are very real and well documented."

"Well, I'm not saying they aren't real, but there comes a time when we have to let go of the past…"

"Did you not just reveal to me that you are a Jew?" asked Malang, his head tilted thoughtfully. "I suggest you be very careful with what you say next lest you find yourself writhing within an embarrassed box of pure hypocrisy of your own making." Arazi glared at Malang with intense hatred.

"Look…!" said the professor, starting to stand.

"OKAY! That looks like time, gentlemen!" said a distressed Umar. "Thank you so much for gracing our humble program with your spirited discussion!" He turned to look into the main camera. "This is Umar Hammoud for *Ferntop Speaks!* Good night!"

* * *

Twelve men sat around a table in a darkened conference room, each watching a personal screen built into the table in front of them. A large picture window showed the skyline of Geneva behind it, the security window's tint creating a sepia-toned effect. Two of the Grey Eminences reached forward to adjust the volume when Jerome Bazzi started raising his voice during the *Ferntop Speaks!* taping they all watched. Each of them wore expensive, tailored suits in various shades of grey, their ties different colors denoting a veiled rank order between them. The twelve sat in thoughtful silence for two minutes once the video stopped.

"His speedy death would have prevented it getting this far," said one in a dark green tie.

"We've been through this before. His martyrdom will give rise to another Black Panther Party or worse. Do you remember how expensive it was to eradicate THAT noise?" said a thin-framed one in a bowler hat and cane.

"All attempts to talk him down and neutralize his propaganda have failed. He has the confident convictions of the true believer. It's like talking to a mad man."

"Not all attempts," said bowler hat. "What's missing from his file is interception by the rose court."

"He's one of these Black Liberation trollops gone rogue. For a century the rose court has practically been a part of his DNA."

"I see no actual evidence that he is actively espousing those points as it hasn't been part of his rhetoric conspicuously. The fact that he leans so heavily into organized religion should be your first clue." A beat of silence from the group broken by a clearing throat noise.

"Some among the lower ranks of the roses do stubbornly hold onto their religions."

"This one is different. We'll send a dedicated team to reinforce the Manifesto's tenets. Perhaps they will manage to loosen his grip upon both this 'New People' mania and on the activist group he's so enamored with."

"And if it fails?"

"We'll table the termination option."

* * *

The chill of late October found Malang avoiding the outdoor festivals to return to the warm interior spaces of the Cyprus Trade Center. Usually a sparse crowd, he was delighted to find himself actively engaged during the weekend due to the numerous people seeking him out after listening and watching his media appearances over the last few weeks.

Malang reiterated his position on both his "New People" spiritual charge and joining the ADOS Advocacy Foundation to help the ethnic group reach their goals faster to a game crowd, pointing to three new prints he made to illustrate the concepts. At a rare break, he got his neighbor—an older

Polish immigrant woman writing people's names on a single grain of rice—to keep an eye on his booth while he went to the restroom. When Malang returned, she acted just as surprised as he to find a single red rose laying across his printed ADOS materials. He looked at it for a few seconds, his mind going through the possible messages that it could have been attempting to convey, then set it aside confident that whoever it belonged to would return for the follow up.

At length, a tanned, but light-skinned elderly Black man strolled over with his hands in his pockets. Standing only about 5ft 6in with balding grey hair, he wore a tan suit and a Dashiki print tie.

"Hey! Aren't you 'Elder' Jackey Leonard?" asked Malang with an appropriate amount of surprise. The older gentleman lit up at the recognition and approached for the obligatory dap.

"What's goin' on, Young Blood? I see you doin' ya thang! A'right nah! I see ya!"

"What in the world are you doing at Cyprus, sir?" Malang asked. "Were you visiting the Democratic Party booth or something?"

"Naw, I came to see YOU," said the 'Elder,' with a sweeping gesture at Malang's prints. "Members of my staff showed me some of them clips that's been goin' viral. You be givin' them honkies a hard time, man! Gaaaaaaddamn! Got 'em runnin'!" The

'Elder' reached in to give Malang more dap as they laughed. "I wanted to come see you personally to give you an invitation to come on by my office. We can use a talented brother like you. I think these, uh, ADOS folk can only get you so far. What you need is to partner with us and these white radicals so we can work to beat back this capitalism, you see what I'm sayin'? That's the real problem." The 'Elder' trailed off as he watched Malang, who had abruptly stopped smiling and studied the old man warily. The 'Elder' reached into his inner coat pocket. "Listen, imma, uh, give you my card. You call me, hear? You call me! We got a position customized just for you. You know, you remind me of them cats I founded the ORIGINAL Black Panther Party with, you dig? You got that same spirit as them brothers and I had. I think we can work together and..."

"Sir, are you the one who left this rose here?"

"Huh? Naw. Naw, that wasn't me. Somebody leaving roses on your table. That's funny. I'on go around given roses to dudes, y'dig? Naw, it wasn't me. You call me. You hear? We can go places together! To the TOP! A'right now!" The 'Elder' reached back in to give some more dap, but Malang's new standoffish coldness now made the greeting awkward. "A'right now, imma get on the road, but you make sure you call me!"

Malang watched the old man walk off down the flea market's row for a few seconds and then looked down at the business card he held. The graphics made it look like a used car dealership flyer, he thought. Which pretty much reflected how the old dude was sounding. He set the card next to the rose and turned back to the crowd.

If he wouldn't have said anything negative about ADOS, thought Malang, he might have reeled him into whatever his clumsy trap was. As Generation-X, Malang was indoctrinated into an exaggerated veneration of those civil rights era relics... the survivors of the F.B.I.'s "Black Messiah" assassination protocols led by that psychopath J. Edgar Hoover. The fact that they survived that era at all, and were the second and third tier leaders in those groups the establishment considered so much a threat, actually should be a suspicious thing. The #ADOS movement is the real thing and for that guy to dismiss it while name-dropping the old civil rights Black Liberation organizations every time he talks is another suspicious point. Who is 'Elder' Jackey Leonard REALLY outside of the marketing campaign his "white radical" handlers put together?

Lost in his thoughts, Malang barely noticed the crowd forming around his table. An overweight white guy with an unkept beard, shoulder-length blond hair and a black t-shirt and jeans gestured to get his attention. "Sir? Sir, are these for sale?" he asked, pointing at the prints.

"Hm? Oh. Yes, they are."

"Ah. That's a little disappointing. Your messaging is really powerful for you to be caught up in that capitalism stuff. It's good work though." Malang's eyes narrowed instinctively and he studied the would-be customer with more focus. Pink foam clogs, various rubber bracelets and political slogan buttons that hit every single liberal-left cause (except ADOS Reparations or even anti-Black American racism) covering his t-shirt completed the costume.

"Is that why you left this rose? To proselytize your anti-capitalism bit at me?" The guy laughed.

"I didn't leave the rose!" he lied.

Malang crossed his arms. "What do you want?"

"Okay, maybe I left the rose. I just don't think you're going about your messaging the right way. Reparations isn't going to fix anything. The best it can do is just make you just another capitalist!"

"I don't subscribe to your spectrum of leftist ideologies, dude. All I care about is my ethnic group being made whole – closing the racial wealth gap by the government providing the long-withheld Reparatory Justice I am owed. That's all. I don't give a crap about whatever Karl Marx and whoever else over there went on about. After one hundred years of being affiliated with your infiltrating, colluding, spectrum political cults, my group is now worse off than we were during jim crow. Without exaggeration, the more I think about you, the angrier I get. Get this rose off my table."

The guy sheepishly walked over and plucked the rose stem up, held the bulb up to smell it as he backed away and stopped about five feet. Then he stepped forward with his right hand out in a handshake pose. "Listen, let's start all over from scratch, okay? My name's Stephen. I apologize."

"Are you still a socialist, communist, democratic socialist, et cetera?"

"Uhhh, y-yeah…"

"Then, nah. I don't want to shake your hand. I don't trust you."

"Okay, that's rude," said Stephen, wiping the rejected hand on his thigh and putting it behind his back. He brought it forward again and held the rose with it.

"Telling me my people don't need what we need and to instead continue to waste time with you patronizing, paternalizing, sabotaging clowns for another hundred years is rude," snarled Malang.

"Look, I don't get what your problem is, man! We all agree that the problem in the world is capitalism and its excesses!" said Stephen, bringing the rose bulb back up to his nose.

"'We' all don't agree with any such a thing. Karl Marx and his buddies and acolytes are no source of truth for me. Your ideologies have done nothing but blow smoke up my people's butts while the whole thing turned out to be yet another white supremacist scam. Whenever my people enjoyed a piece of land-property ownership and living off the fruits of their labors in anything close to the competitive open free markets that capitalism requires to function, they thrived, and were able to build a piece of wealth and something like happiness. It is you who has helped strip that piece of happiness from us to turn us into test dummy lab rats in your filthy red commie schemes, setting me back closer and closer to the shackles of chattel! Get that crap out of my face!" Malang shouted, pointing up the row. Stephen watched him for a beat with a stoic face, shook his head and started walking away.

"Peace & love™, brother. It doesn't have to be like this. Obviously, your mind is poisoned by the capitalists so you can't see truth."

"Yeah, okay." Malang probed into his anger to see why that type of figure was so able to push his buttons faster than the clowns on the other side of that racist spectrum. It's not like they *both* weren't gaslighty, insufferable jackasses. It's just that the left is the one always pretending to be

ADOS' buddy while exploiting & plundering in the classic sense. As bad as lineage-based racism is in general, it's the icing of hypocrisy that takes that foul cake over the top for Malang, he thought.

The crowd ebbed and flowed into the early afternoon, keeping Malang engaged and sharp with their questions and responses, both the interested and those who expressed resentment at the very idea of an economically whole and competitively equal American Descendants of Slavery. Conscious of his earlier loss of patience and anger with the Stephen guy, Malang worked to keep his tone neutral so as not to 'taint the witness' of his support of the movement. How things looked and sounded on the surface often determined whether people would take a message seriously or not; the worthiness won't even be considered if the outer packaging isn't right. It didn't matter what Malang thought of this fact—as Margaret would point out *ad nauseam* in the early days of traveling this road—it is what it is. He didn't need to compromise in his actual messaging, but he would have to bend when it came to how it was presented. Malang certainly didn't want to inadvertently turn people away from the ADOS Advocacy Foundation because he let people get under his skin and didn't maintain his poise out of what honestly only came down to pride and ego.

A young woman asked him how much for a print. Malang told her and she promptly started digging into her pocketbook. She was brown-skinned, a shade darker than he, and almost Malang's height. She was dressed conservatively, but her curves were noticeable. She was very attractive. She handed Malang the money and looked into his eyes, holding his gaze for a beat with her lips pursed. She looked away coyly, paused, then tossed her hair dramatically and looked back at him with a confident tilt of her head. Malang smiled and shook his head slightly.

"So, what is it about the print that speaks to you?" he asked. The print depicted two figures representing the 1% grifter class exploiting a distressed ADOS couple. Cash was being siphoned from the couple onto the 1% class side of the image.

"I like that it unapologetically tells the truth about end-state capitalism," she said. "We definitely need more of that out here."

"I'm sorry. My name is Malang."

"Pleased to meet you, Malang. I'm Yona."

"Please to meet you, too. What do you mean by 'end-state capitalism,' please?"

"Well, it's no secret that the excesses of the 1% billionaire class, with their trademark 'haves vs have-nots' assault upon the people, is where capitalism inevitably leads, no matter what the original good intentions may or may not have been."

Malang paused, noticing the same anger rising up that he felt earlier when he snapped at that blond clown. Then he saw the small lapel pin on Yona's trendy blazer. It was a rose. "I think the actual secret—since the knowledge of it is rarely discussed—is that 'capitalism' the system doesn't inevitably lead anywhere," said Malang slowly, carefully regulating his tone. "It's actually a certain class of humans and their propensity for an obsessive 'bigness' pursuit of Über-greed, that inevitably strives to reach the heights of those excesses whenever they are allowed to do so by unscrupulous officials and lax laws. In other words, the problem is the dedicated criminal class among us that the laws of civilization were created in the first place to discourage and bring to account when they cross the line."

"Are you saying that capitalism isn't the problem? I can't believe that," said Yona shaking her head. "Our Black leaders pointed out again and again…"

"They pointed out only what they were reciting off of those communist ideology tracts they had memorized. That didn't mean what they were regurgitating was magically true."

"So, you're a capitalist?"

"I agree that American citizens should be allowed

to own assets, to build wealth, to make contracts, to contract with the U.S. government for lucrative grants & low-interest loan services and to be able to fairly compete in the regulated open free markets as economic equals to white people."

"This isn't about race…"

"It's about race in America as it has always been. How could it not be? The obscene wealth of the West was built by the economic exploitation and plunder of a specific identity group targeted along racial phenotype to benefit an identity group favored along racial phenotype. That is the nature of the economic issues in the USA for lo, these four centuries. Locking my people…"

"OUR people." Yona put her hands on her hips and struck a sassy pose as she held Malang's gaze again with a knowing smirk.

"…our people out of access to the wealth-building ownership class isn't 'end-state capitalism' because the nature of the grift is anti-competition. The American Descendants of Slavery, the Black American former slave class ethnic group, isn't allowed to fairly compete as economic equals with our ideological foes. Capitalism is ALL about competition as its lifeblood, and as soon as that competition is cut off it is no longer capitalism. What the hoarding monopoly of the 1% grifter class represents, is end-state communism." A look of irritation came across

Yona's face and she stopped trying to flirt.

"Pardon me? What... what odd definition of capitalism are you using exactly?"

"From the formal economic glossary definition. I have zero reason to go around pretending anything Marx put forth is anything of universal truth. About anything." Yona looked up at him with a slightly furrowed brow, tossed the hair out of her face and pointed to her print.

"Were you going to wrap that, or...?"

"Oh! Yes. Hold on, please." Malang put her package together while she watched him, still frowning slightly, with her arms folded. She nodded her head towards his wedding ring.

"You must drive your wife crazy with all that stubbornness, huh?" Malang looked at her and smiled.

"My wife and I are on one accord, ma'am. Not that I'm not stubborn sometimes, but we are on one accord in all areas where it counts the most. Including the current topic of discussion."

"It's not current anymore. Have a nice day," said Yona, with a cool tone in her voice. Malang waved, she turned away and walked up the row, all her curves poppin' to the beat of her strut. Malang shook his head and turned away to catch the eye of a Black man watching him with a knowing look. Malang shrugged with a lopsided grin and they shared a laugh.

* * *

Special Agent Phillip Konde read aloud from his personal laptop, "In order to be successful in this #ADOS movement, we must have the ability to inspire the people to do the tedious work after they have finished working for the day. We do that by painting the picture of a glorious post-Reparations life for the American Descendants of Slavery, an abundant life of wealth and security." Special Agent Konde sat thoughtfully considering the *Breaking-Brown* newsletter message from Yvette Carnell. His deep dive into these materials… the data-driven content of the two #ADOS founders and their library of recommendations… gave him a new appreciation for this ethnic group, long-suffering as they have been in this land of milk & honey. A land of milk & honey for everyone but them thus far. He had taken them for granted in the way the immigrant class is want to do, little different than how they think of their own countrymen left behind to live in their own challenging squalor conditions. For ADOS it was different; conditioned for generations to be a wealthless bottom caste, every time they did rise up to seize their rightful portion of their own country, they were violently pushed back down again. The record is clear on that score. Special Agent Konde gained new insight particularly in how Malang Flathill came across when he talked about these bullets. At first, he thought it was a cheap smug arrogance, but now he realized it was the firm conviction of someone who spoke from the position of immovable truth. Combined with his theist faith walk, it was no wonder Malang spoke with an (often insufferable) authority that seemed to belie his humble station in life. 'Wokeness' tends to do that to people, Konde sniffed.

His mission phone buzzed. "Yeah. Konde here."

"It's Director Raye. Are you alright?"

"Oh, yes. I'm fine. No worries." Konde probed around in his psyche to assure himself he wasn't just responding on auto-pilot. "Right as rain, as they say." Director Raye's tone of voice gave away that he seemed satisfied enough and didn't require any additional convincing.

"I have a snuff mission for you. I mean, if you're up to it. I don't need you uncharacteristically falling apart on me when I think everything is fine. You tell me if you aren't up to it," he quipped.

"No, I'm fine, Chris. What do you have?"

"The bosses just want this one gone. They don't care about the niceties. They say that, but we both know we don't need any more shit and this one is already sensitive. I want you to make it look like an accident if you can, but if it's too much…"

"No, no. I told you, I'm fine. Whatever you need."

"I need you to get that Flathill asshole out of our hair. Tell me when it's done."

"Are we supposed to be talking about this part over the phone?" asked Konde quietly.

"Are you serious?" responded Raye with a chuckle. "It's just those damned former slave blackies versus the whole world; nobody cares about them. I can say whatever the hell I want about them in front of an audience of millions and no one will stand up for them. Someone might pretend to care, but then use the hoopla to redirect support towards our guys." Director Raye laughed and then cut it off. "You know as well as I they have no power; the white racist aristocracy has spent the last 150 years making sure of that. Now I need you to get rid of this damned guy before they GET some power and then suddenly, we can't talk about them like this anymore. Capisce?"

"Yes, sir," said Konde coldly. The director disconnected, leaving Special Agent Konde sitting at the hotel room's desk feeling his heart pound in his chest. He slowly lowered the phone and looked down at his lap simultaneously.

It's okay, he thought. You have options. You can either blindly follow the F.B.I. Director's order and assure your place in the pit of hell, or you can do as you personally vowed to do and use your skills to protect Malang. Not really much of a choice when you think about it, he thought, widening his eyes and running his hands over his head. Konde stood up and paced in the room to get his thoughts flowing. He abruptly paused and looked back at his laptop. He put it away, pulled out his Bureau-issue and opened a memo template with F.B.I. letterhead.

"Dear colleagues of Black American identity, you who are of the American Descendants of Slavery," he typed. His fingers hovered over the keys briefly and then the memo started coming to life.

An hour later, Special Agent Konde had reread the memo a dozen times, carefully editing, tweaking, rewriting, until it was finally as good as he believed it could get. If he could send it only to the ADOS personnel in the F.B.I. he would. Instead, he settled for sending it to the entire Bureau. He promptly took the batteries out of his devices, packed his things and hit the streets.

* * *

Seven minutes after Special Agent Konde sent his memo through the F.B.I.'s email distro list, Director Raye added him to his new snuff list. "I don't give a shit. You call me when he's found," he snapped at the Special Agent on the phone. When the director hung up the call, a familiar headache started pounding at his temples and he immediately unclenched his teeth, relieving the self-inflicted pressure.

Director Raye didn't know what was worse… Konde's betrayal, or the fact that he was no doubt writing that damned email while he was assuring him he was fine. He reread the weird-assed memo. Addressed specifically to the Black American ethnic group employed in the Bureau, it was both a one-man apology for the Black immigrant class's contribution to the post-1965 Immigration and Nationality Act sabotage of ADOS group uplift, as well as a heartfelt plea for them to turn their attention to this ADOS Advocacy Foundation and put in the vital movement work so their group could finally be free in this land… "of theirs." Director Raye shook his head and laughed with a bitter sardonic bark, rubbing his hand across his sweaty face. Konde has turned into a damned true believer blackie-lover. The director contemplated putting this stupid piece of shit out of his confused misery himself.

Director Raye groaned aloud when the phone rang, showing the tell-tale row of pound symbols.

"Yes, your Grey Eminences," he croaked.

"Is he dead?"

"Uh, no. No, he appears to have turned one of our Special Agents to his cause. The agent sent out some pro-blackie propaganda through the Bureau's distro... the entire Federal Government is abuzz. I have agents getting it done though. We'll get..."

An abrupt *click* and dial tone. Director Raye sat back, looked out of his tinted office window and rubbed his hands together.

* * *

"Our task, per the two founders," said Malang to a young ADOS couple standing in front of his Cyprus Trade Center table. "is to organize the people to take on our government, which isn't fun. As Yvette described it, it's the un-sexy drudgery of movement work, but it must be done. The hardest part of it is convincing the wealthless bottom caste—who already spend up the majority of their time just keepin' their head above the water—to spend what little time they have left to perform that drudgery. So, the very last thing ADOS needs, are slimy, pseudo-movements and fake organizations pretending to do the work, and recruiting our people into impotent 'Diversity, Equity & Inclusion' corporate roles that eat up all their time making them think they are doing the work. PowerPoint slides and videoconference group calls espousing 'implicit bias' and 'POC/BIPOC' drivel, along with endless fake protected classes that were designed to further economically enrich white people while burying the ADOS struggle in fake 'post-racial' partisan rhetoric." The couple thanked Malang, promised to check out the ADOS Advocacy Foundation website and took the print they purchased with them down the flea market row. Malang saw Special Agent Konde watching him with a look on his face he couldn't decipher.

"Hey, Bud. Peace," Konde offered with what Malang could only interpret as shyness.

"Peace. How are you doing?"

"I'm good."

"You come for another shot at the title?" asked Malang, with a mischievous grin. The agent laughed and waved him off.

"Naw, I don't want no trouble! I didn't come for that smoke, not this time. I do need to talk to you though. It's important."

"About what?" Malang frowned. Konde approached the table rapidly. Malang instinctively put his right leg back in guard position, but the agent only put a folded piece of paper in his hand.

"I'll be in touch," he said quietly and disappeared down the row.

7

Running in Plain Sight

Jay Williams collected the folders spread out on the conference table from the meeting.

The Democratic National Committee leaders met with key constituency heads for the morning's 9 o'clock. Jay dutifully took notes and provided source files when asked. As the party filed out of Conference Room Alpha, he held the folder pile close to his chest, his bald head held high to enable him to see underneath the glasses he wore. They were fine for reading text close up, but useless for looking at distance. He wore them anyway because they made a decent disguise for this role he allowed himself to be put in, the picture he painted with his head up that way noticeably disarming, putting his colleagues at ease almost immediately; almost all of them treated him like a harmless teddy bear. This was a valuable trait for a 6ft 6in, almost 500 lb Black American man. He stopped in front of the Chairman's office, the latter still settling in at his desk.

"Mr. Harrison, will that be all?" Jay asked, deliberately uptalking in a sing-song voice.

"Oh, that's fine, Jay. Go on to lunch. We can manage without you for an hour, I think. Keep your phone on you," said Chairman Harrison, this last with a wink. Jay chuckled and thanked him, the trousers to his black suit making a swishing noise as he hurriedly switched his way down the hallway. He dumped the files on the desk in his little cubbyhole (even immersed in this role, he refused to call this shit an "office"), and headed on out to the Washington D.C. streets.

Jay's favorite diner was owned by a Polish man, Mr. Korfanty, who was also from Philadelphia. Jay had struck up a friendship of sorts with the sometimes gruff immigrant's son, and if he was in the mood, he would handmake Jay a Philly cheese steak sandwich himself. This was simply the best because when Mr. Korfanty made it, it tasted exactly like home... Jay's last remaining anchor to his old life.

To his disappointment, Mr. Korfanty wasn't in today. Phooey, he thought, mentally still in character. Jay ordered the super grilled cheese and pulled out his phone when he felt the buzz. He smiled. Those folks couldn't find their own butts without him. Jay paused in mid-sip of his orange juice, the straw hovering fractions of a millimeter from his lower lip when he saw the row of pound symbols on his phone.

"Yes, your Grey Eminences. How may I serve you?" he said at a near whisper, sweat immediately beading on his dark brown skin. Jay turned into the corner booth he sat in, his back hunched in a rounded turtle shell.

"Jayson. It's important that you don't disappointment us. We've had quite enough disappointments in the last few months. Has word of this Malang Flathill reached you?"

"It has."

"Please remove him from my planet. Choose whomsoever you wish to partner with you and get it done. Sooner rather than later. The F.B.I. has failed us and failed and failed again."

"The CIA will not fail, your Grey Eminences. On my word." Jay slipped the phone back into his pocket at the disconnecting click. He looked down at his food as if he had never seen it before, then gathered it together in a heap and quickly walked out of the door.

* * *

The Konde Memo, as it was called, quickly spread like wildfire, first through the Bureau, and then by word-of-mouth throughout the other agencies of the Federal Government. In less than a week, it had leaked into the general population, its message igniting a positive awareness of the #ADOS movement among the Black American ethnic group it served that proved to overpower the steady stream of negative propaganda and false narratives the group's ideological foes projected almost from day one. The potency of a formal apology from a Black immigrant Federal Government intelligence agent, who not only commended the virtues of the ADOS Advocacy Foundation on behalf of its members, but it also admitted the many wrongs the Bureau inflicted upon ADOS over the decades in order to support the dominance of white supremacist racketeering structures in the post-civil rights era, could not be denied.

The memo ended with an odd religious/spiritual plea—linking to the blog of a Black "art activist" Malang Flathill—imploring the ADOS ethnic group to recognize that they were indeed the "raised up New People" whom the One God warned the two Semite nations of in both of their holy books, who would replace them for their slipshod religious practices, who would not turn away from the calling the Divine revealed and would walk out the religion of faith in excellence. The surge of calls and queries to join #ADOSAF and do the movement work was spectacular, rivaling the rabid growth of the original Nation of Islam once the charismatic Malcolm X became a public spokesman.

* * *

The Flathill's burgundy sedan zipped along Interstate-75 northbound towards Lorette, Mishigamaa making good time. With seven hours of the ten the GPS calculated it would take to get to the Upper Peninsula town behind them, Margaret only had to ask Malang to slow down twice. Olivia was fast asleep in her car seat, sounding like a mini-buzzsaw, the hum of the car's motor affecting her like a sleep-aid drug.

The note Special Agent Konde handed Malang that morning briefly explained that he was in grave danger. Malang met with the man he only knew as Phillip in a public place, where in hushed tones the taller man explained that he was a federal agent (flashed his badge) and he was trying to help. The Federal Bureau of Investigation had been ordered to eliminate Malang in what could only be considered classic anti-ADOS lynching motives. Special Agent Konde provided the key to the safehouse in Lorette and instructed Malang he couldn't tell anyone where they were going. No one at all.

Malang decided to take the agent at face value; he didn't like the idea of gambling with his family's lives (what if it was true?), and what was wrong with a little family getaway? Nothing. Phillip said the place was really nice.

When the GPS said they were only a mile away from the safehouse, the Flathills pulled into the parking lot of a burger joint, got out and stretched their legs (the couple noticed that Lorette was at least 10 degrees colder than Chocolate City was this late-October), grabbed the sleeping baby, then went into the restaurant to refresh themselves and grab a bite to eat.

* * *

Jay Williams and his hand-picked partner, Terry Leland, watched the Flathills exit I-75 from Terry's satellite monitor in the back of a charcoal gray utility van. They lagged behind the family about twenty miles. Jay dug into both the Flathill and Konde files, and had a good idea of where Malang was taking his family. Too little, too late, Jay thought. He had met his partner about fifteen years ago during a cyber surveillance training they attended, with Terry definitely the more into that type of work between the two. Jay preferred the interpersonal field work over sitting behind a desk at Agency HQ or wherever, staring into a bunch of monitors all day. The fact that Terry loved that though, made him a no-brainer pick for Jay's network.

* * *

A dark green taxi pulled up in front of a boarded-up decrepit building on Chocolate City's east side. Special Agent Konde approached, looked around and reached for the door handle. Just out of his peripheral vision, a steely low-crouching figure came running up on his right, too quick for Konde to react, and pushed a hard object under his rib cage.

"Thanks for getting us the cab, Phil," said Jay in a friendly voice. "That's what's up." The two slid into the backseat; Konde stoic-faced, Jay grinning like a delighted child. Jay gave the driver terse directions and pushed the pistol barrel into Konde's rib, nodding his head towards the road ahead.

"I'm just trying to see if I recognize you," said Konde, mimicking Jay's friendly demeanor.

"Stuff like that will just get you in trouble, Phillip," said Jay, putting enough extra emphasis on the last syllable to make a wet *pop* sound. "Trust me, nobody wants that."

"Well, from my poi—! Erk..." Another push into Konde's rib silenced him, accompanied by a low hissing "shhhhhhhh" from Jay.

"That's enough now. Relax."

A closely following Jay directed Konde up a flight of steps behind an abandoned bar. Jay provided an irregular knock and Terry Leland opened the door, quickly pulling Konde inside. A stiff pistol blow behind the ear and Konde dropped to the floor in a heap. The two CIA agents half carried, half dragged the unconscious Konde to a back bedroom, handcuffed his hands behind his back and closed the door. Terry caught a look from Jay, nodded and dialed a number on a burner phone.

"We got your boy. I don't see what exactly is so 'special' about you lames, but whatever." He chuckled, provided the other party with the address and disconnected.

When Konde came to, he investigated to determine if there was any pain other than that raging in his head. No. He shifted position to allow the blood to flow and the feeling returned to his left hand. Okay, now there's some more pain, he thought. When the dexterity of that hand returned, he performed his handcuff escape trick, a skill he picked up back when he assumed F.B.I. Special Agent would be a lot more Hollywood glamorous and exciting – not that this wasn't exciting in its own way. The fact that Bureau life wasn't that exciting is why he was so complacent to allow that big, black bald goon to catch him unawares like that. Or so he told himself.

Konde tossed the cuffs aside and got to his feet, rubbing the bruise behind his ear. He eased up close to the door, alert for any sounds. He opened the door, noted the significant change in light quality – how long was he out…? – and checked the rooms, but he was alone. He left, moving quickly down the steps in the cold air. Ducking into the alley, he worked to put the battery back into his phone. He had instructed Malang to take the battery out of his and not to contact anyone. He sort of hoped he listened to him, sort of not. The automated voice told him the other party's phone wasn't in service. Konde nodded and snatched his own battery back out and kept on the move. Moments later, the F.B.I. showed up at the apartment to fetch him from the room.

* * *

On a clean Lorette side street, the Flathill's sedan

turned up into a private drive lane, flanked on each side by 9ft tall, manicured hedge bushes. Special Agent Konde instructed Malang not to drive to the main front entrance of the safehouse, but to go in from the back. Malang bristled and contemplated whether he would follow those instructions to the tee; Konde being an immigrant may not understand the nature of the inherent indignity he asked of him based on the history of ADOS. Now that he had arrived, in an alien side of his home state with family in tow, Malang decided this wasn't the time to be overly-militant "blickety-black" petty over trifles just for the abstract principle.

"Hashtag: 'pick your battles,'" he said in a low voice.

"What did you say?" asked Margaret immediately.

"Just reminding myself to pick my battles. Not every topic is worth walking all the way down to the ground in an epic four-hour debate."

"Honey, I thought you were going to leave work behind for a few days? Clear your mind, please, and be present. Let's just do family time."

"You're right. Sorry. Livvie, you okay?" he asked aloud, looking at the baby's face in the rear view mirror. Olivia baby-talked an acknowledgment that Malang and Margaret decided to take at face value. "We're almost there. You're doin' good."

The hedge-flanked driveway let them out underneath a sunshade awning, with a marked, six slot parking lot area. Malang parked at the end, right up next to the backdoor. To his quiet relief and a tingle of excitement, the key worked and they went in.

After about 20 minutes of exploring, the couple realized that the 'safehouse' was more like a 'safe-mansion,' and they retreated back to where they started to bring in their things from the car before they ended up lost.

The two determined which suite of rooms they were going to take for themselves and Malang dutifully carried their bags to the bedroom while Margaret cleaned up the baby. Afterwards, they returned to their exploring, with a laser-focus on the kitchen.

"Look, honey," said Margaret with an awed tone. Malang followed her pointing finger to the sky-high, hallway ceiling, massive portraits of mysterious figures lining the walls. Margaret hurried forward towards an ornate lamp table with some sort of printed material in a clear holder sat invitingly atop. The brochures described the mansion itself, informing them that it was built in the neoclassical architectural style and, at 13,000 square feet, was the largest mansion in the Mishigamaa Upper Peninsula. With a new appreciation for their impromptu family getaway retreat, the couple lingered to read about a dozen of the identification plaques under the portraits, each a piece of the haunting history commemorated at the Lorette Manor Inn.

The couple squealed when they finally entered the kitchen, tingling excitement washing over Malang's head and neck in waves, when they discovered the pantry and refrigerator fully stocked. Olivia caught their excitement like a viral contagion and squeaked & squealed her toddler songs in the background of the mini-feast the family set to prepare. Malang and Margaret promised one another they would clean up as they went along, for an amused Malang to discover that he was cleaning up as Margaret went along… her skillful hands preparing several dishes at once, most of them Malang's personal favorites.

* * *

A charcoal gray van parked up the road on the opposite side from the Lorette Manor Inn. After about 15 minutes, Jay and Terry came out and briskly walked across until they were swallowed up into the darkness of the hedge-flanked side road. Both of them wore black backpacks; Jay carried a large gasoline can. As they trekked up the lonely, dark road, Jay began to sing quietly to himself, regularly jerking his head to shake off the bead of sweat pooling under his philtrum, despite the near freezing temperature. Upon reaching the end of the road, they darted across the well-lit parking lot to settle in under the bushes facing the suite the Flathills had chosen.

Jay removed his backpack and carefully, methodically pulled out his tools. Terry watched for ten minutes and then pulled out a few of his own. When he was done, Jay sat up crossed-legged and started pressing buttons on his wrist-watch. Then he looked towards the mansion and slowly closed his eyes. In less than a minute, his breathing changed and his head tilted slightly towards his lap. Terry watched his partner for a minute and shook his head.

* * *

The Flathill family finished their meal, cleaned up and returned to the suite to bed down for the night. Malang patrolled their self-designated area, making sure all the doors were locked, hoping it would calm him down since he had been feeling excitable and keyed up since they arrived. He would have liked to give his little family this kind of experience all the time, he thought, a tingle rippling around his face.

"Thank you, Lord," Malang muttered absently and headed back to the bedroom.

"Look at this," Margaret said, sitting on the edge of the bed holding a tiny hand as a giggling Olivia bounced up and down. "She's not even sleepy!"

"She did all of that sleeping in the car," said Malang. He scooped his daughter up into his arms and walked around the huge bedroom rubbing her back and singing softly into her neck. A little over 20 minutes later she was asleep, however deeply. The couple showered and made love in the enormous bed.

Exhausted from the long drive, an irritated Malang nevertheless lied on his back wide awake still, listening to the sounds of his family breathing. He slipped out of his wife's arms and went to shower, marveling at the ornate attention to detail. He thanked the One God for the experience and said, "Oh, my Lord! But a tiny fraction of the splendor will be waiting for those who believe in the gardens of paradise! Please know that I believe in you, me and my family, and we pray for your Mercy that we may be counted among the ranks of the righteous!"

Malang slipped on a pair of sweats and a t-shirt, and retraced his steps from the night's security patrol. Occasionally he would try a window latch or a door handle to ensure they were secured. After he had made one full circuit around the suites, he glanced at the large time piece on the front room (living room…?) counter. Twenty minutes. Wow. And that's just one suite, he thought.

On his second circuit around the suite, Malang allowed his mind to wander, returning to work themes. The "drudgery" work required for an effective movement that #ADOS leadership described is exactly what the ethnic group needed to focus on in order to achieve our political goals, he mused. He remembered in his studies, how the Jewish community used exactly such work – "writing, the phone calls, the reading" – to establish the modern nation state of Israel. And this was done without the tools of the Internet at their disposal! All ADOS wants is to get policies passed in our own government, not create a whole new sovereign country, and we have better tools with a wider reach. In scripture, the One God said to seek His help with "patient perseverance and prayer, for God is with those who patiently persevere," pointedly placing greater emphasis over consistency & fortitude than over prayer to have God's All-Mighty Power in the favor of those who believe. Malang's face tingled as he prayed in that moment that his people, the American Descendants of Slavery, saw the Path and how it aligned so well with their own worthy political cause.

Do the difficult and tedious drudgery work of the movement with patient perseverance IN THE NAME OF GOD without complaint, and if it be God's Will, we will win through to – as Yvette called it – the promised land of an abundant, post-Reparations life as full U.S. citizens.

"That's how we will win," said Malang aloud, his eyes welling up. "Amen."

* * *

Neither Jay nor Terry noticed the shadow of their primary target walking pass the window above them as they scurried over from the well-manicured bushes of the Lorette Manor Inn to hunch against the wall.

"Come on," whispered Jay, running over to the nearest door. He reached into a cargo pocket to pull out a small, deceptively light piece of metal – flat with two parallel grooves on one side. The other side had *Bully-Snap!*® embedded in the metal. Jay slid the object onto the door's middle hinge, gestured for Terry to go the opposite way and ran over to the next door. Terry pulled out the same device and ran to duplicate the task.

When all the doors were securely fastened from

the outside, trapping the sleeping family within, Jay began pouring gasoline on the wall outside of the suite's bedroom. He darted off, pouring along the base as he went. When he turned the corner, Terry set the fuel ablaze and retreated to the bushes. Jay joined him almost eight minutes later.

Malang mulled over the implications of ADOS agreeing to take on the "New People" idea. Of course the Hebrew Israelite crowd would be mad, but whatever. Why would they ever want to take on that identity in the first place, he wondered. The historical circumstances behind the "lost tribes" concept were not exactly honorable – both wandering in the wilderness for 40 years and having the Solomonic Era Temples sacked & looted were circumstances born of willful disobedience to that group's Creator. By contrast, the 230 years of legal bondage and the subsequent 150 years of accrued lineage-based discriminatory practices were imposed upon ADOS through the evils of unreasonable men, whose love for hoarding money just for themselves trumped any decency they pretended to project into the world.

He paused in his thoughts… the light quality had changed dramatically; the shadows in the room jumping and dancing. Malang ran over to a window and saw flames blazing up from the base of the house! He ran towards the bedroom calling for his wife to wake up.

Malang burst into the room which was already thickening with smoke. He dove onto the bed shaking Margaret.

"Bae, get up! There's a fire! We gotta get out of here!!" He snatched a thick coverlet and wrapped the baby in it. Margaret, wrapped in a thick blanket plodded towards the door with a hurt and stunned look on her face. Malang quickly turned the lock on the first outside door but it wouldn't open! He wasted a bit of time pushing and kicking on it, then moved to the next. He and Margaret coughing as he kept the baby fully wrapped in the coverlet. The double-snap of the next door's opening lock also failed to herald their escape.

"Bae, what's happening?!" shouted Margaret, signaling she was now fully awake. A rippling tingle crept up Malang's back at the sound of her voice.

"It's okay, we're getting out of here. Stay with me." They moved to the next door and Margaret took the baby from him.

"Please, God. Please," Malang chanted as he turned the next door's lock. It also refused to budge. Malang abruptly turned, seized a heavy wooden chair he walked over to one of the huge windows and heaved it at the glass as hard as he could. The loud *boom* made Margaret jump, but the chair fell to the floor without making a single nick in the glass.

"Okay, c'mon. C'mon," he said, guiding his family to the next door. Both he and Margaret began praying aloud; Olivia beginning to cry. All the windows were bright with dancing flame. Malang wondered what it would look like on the other side of whichever door finally opened, and pushed the thought aside. Right now he would be glad to deal with that hurdle. He turned the next lock, pushed down the handle and at the moment he felt the door refuse to give, Malang's entire field of vision was replaced by the *veil between realities* and the glowing portal of the 'third eye.'

Through this voracious vision of second sight, he could still see the texture of the door through the portal, more detailed and richer than he could ever see with his two mortal eyes of first sight. As he stared, a Word began to form in the door… four letters… one-by-one in a bright glow. When the fourth letter was completed, the brightness dimmed and Malang returned from his vision to the burning house. He quickly reached out his right hand to trace the letters as he uttered the Word in a medium-toned voice before the vision completely faded and the door instantly opened! The family gratefully poured out into the freezing cold clear air, thanking the One God for His favor. Coughing in fits, Malang took Olivia and the family moved away from the flames around towards the front of the house. Malang felt an intense feeling of déjà vu as he glanced over at the burning building.

"Bae! This was my second 'third eye' vision! This is what I saw!" Margaret looked at him in wonder, pulling the blanket closer around her. "It was exactly like this!"

"Malang, what's going to happen now?" she asked him in a pleading voice. "We can't stay out here! It's freezing!"

"No, we can't." Malang paused listening intensely. He thought to detect the sound of sirens in the distance, but he wasn't sure. He wished he would have grabbed the car keys before they ran out, but he couldn't remember where they were off the top of his head. He didn't think it was realistic that he would have been able to search them out in time, they barely made it out as it was. His mind wanted to linger on the miraculous fourth 'third eye' vision event, but he refused to give himself that luxury while his family was still in danger.

"How the hell did you get out of there?!" shouted a confused, loud voice. Malang looked over to his right to see two figures approaching from the hedge line, both holding a two-handed grip on automatic pistols pointed at the ground. "I thought you'd be barbecued by now," said the tall Black one of the two.

"You did this?" Malang, asked with anger in his voice.

"I did, but don't worry. We can still cook the bodies afterwards." Jay nodded towards the burning mansion. His head jerked slightly at the now unmistakable sound of sirens in the distance and he raised his gun to aim right at Malang's head.

"Are you an immigrant?" asked Malang. "At least explain that's why you are a treacherous piece of garbage because we don't have anything in common except shallow melanin tones. Tell me."

"No, but I wish I was," said Jay, focusing his sight-picture dead on the center of Malang's forehead. "I'd take anything on the continent over being the descendant of lazy wretches that the whole damned world spits on."

"Lazy?" snarled Malang with a sneer. "You've been hanging around and listening to these too much." He nodded his head at Terry. Our people were literally worked to death clearing the great forests of North America and then built the great wealth of Western Civilization while we were prevented from building wealth to pass along to our children and children's children. The only people who call us lazy after all we've done are the people who plundered the fruits of our labor and lusted for more and more. Our people are not lazy."

"Yeah, well," said Jay. "I'm familiar with your file. I've read all your stuff. Who do you think you're supposed to be?"

"I am a believer in the Most-High, the Lord and Cherisher of the heavens and earth. I am a proud member of the American Descendants of Slavery, the uncrowned true elite protected class of these United States of America."

"Don't you understand that none of that means anything?!" shouted Jay.

"You think it doesn't mean anything that God is God? Well, that's convenient based on what you just tried to do to my family."

"'Tried to do?' What I'm going to do!"

"Hey, man. How about go ahead and let's get this done and get out of here?" said Terry, gesturing at the Flathills with his gun barrel. "The fire department will be here any minute."

"God is EVERYTHING," said Malang with force. "Everything. The One God is the Source Truth from which all lesser truths emanate. Nothing at all happens lest He wills it. That's the literal opposite of not meaning anything. Your mind is weak. That's why you stand here like this, performing the actions you perform.."

"YOU DON'T KNOW SHIT ABOUT ME!!!"

"I know you are the filthy unrepentant hellbound.

I know that. I know you F.B.I. goons have a long ugly history of warring against my people."

Jay barked a laugh. "I ain't no damned lame-assed G-man. In fact, your boy should be executed by now."

"You said you saw my file. What are you then? The CIA?"

A thirty second pause. "No," Jay croaked.

"Sure."

"Hey, man…!" began Terry as the flashing lights of Lorette public safety vehicles showed along the long hedge bushes. Jay abruptly turned and shot his partner in the head. Margaret screamed. When the body dropped, Jay stood over it and shot it twice more in the head. He reached up, closed off a nostril and blew a ribbon of mucus out of the other into the grass. Malang watched this warily as Jay turned back towards them, nonchalantly holding his pistol in one hand pointed at the ground. He started laughing.

"I don't even know why I did that!" Tears started streaming down his face.

"Maybe you wished you were him. Maybe you wished you were a white man and the idea that you don't have to wish that – that you can be a proud ADOS and finally live a full life conflicted with that in your mind. You know racism as we know it will be over once we are made whole, right?"

"Bullshit. Them crazy motherfuckers will never stop hating us."

"Irrelevant. It's this nationwide, racketeering, organized crime ring we call white supremacy that will be over. The individuals among them will continue to feel whatever they felt when they colluded with the white elites to permanently delegate our enslaved African ancestors to the bondsman class, but the system itself will be destroyed, God willing."

The sirens were loud enough where Malang could barely hear himself, but Jay reacted as if he heard him just fine. He glared at Malang for a beat and then smoothly brought up his pistol to aim at him again. Malang uttered a two syllable Word then a new 'third eye' vision overtook his consciousness. He saw the NAME appear within the portal once more in a flash and Malang traced his finger through the Letters as it faded away. Jay pointed the gun barrel up into the roof of his own mouth just as a fire truck burst out from the hedge-lined side road. His head jerked when the gunshot went off… a spray of white-speckled goo flying up behind him… and as he fell forward, Malang caught the saddest look he had ever seen in his life on Jay's face.

Fire-fighters ran over to the Flathills and Malang turned to hug his family tight, kissing their faces and heads, all the time thanking the One God for

His special favor.

8

EPILOGUE

Personal Record of a 'Third Eye' Vision #5
Malang's Artist Website

My wife said she didn't see anything unusual. She said I just unlocked the door and pushed it open. Likewise, she said the rogue CIA agent had the gun on me and then just shot himself. She said she didn't see me move at all, let alone trace the tetragrammaton Letters in the air the way I described. She didn't hear me utter the NAME aloud either.

I'm just a little disappointed that she wasn't able to see anything of what I saw from the two new 'third eye' visions I described in the previous blog post. It's not that big of a deal, I just wanted to share that special experience with my beloved. These mystical second sight experiences are my gifts of the spirit, designed to continue to guide me on a

Way that is Straight. As I said in previous 'third eye' blogs posts, my job is to stay on the Path, stick to my commitment to my art, fight for my people and don't slip and taint my witness. Staying on the Path is challenging—temptations come at us from every direction—as the fiend in its jealous bitterness told the One God it would do to make us slip up. But when we slip, get up, repent in the Name of God and do it no more. That's the key to winning at life.

Now about this NAME…

Here I thought I was blessed beyond my wildest dreams just to have experienced the opening of the Wisdom Eye of legend! If I thought it was nigh-impossible for me to be gifted with such a thing, how much more fantastic is it that the Lost Name of God was revealed to me??? I am grateful beyond words, and yet all I've been doing lately is thanking The Most-High again and again.

I know you want me to tell you what it is, what the NAME looks like, duplicate it in my art, or something. Naturally, I expect you to ask, whether you believe me or not.

The answer is a definitive "No."

If it was like that, then obviously the One God would have made sure His prophets had kept the NAME among the people so that it would never have gotten lost. This is clearly a personal gift—as are all gifts of the spirit—that requires me to guard it from corruption to prevent just any ninny from blabbing it about and causing all kinds of mischief in the land. I am not one to give up precious secrets so easily.

What I would like to do is describe around the NAME. I won't reveal the actual Word, but I will say this: It was not in Hebrew. It was not in Arabic.

It was the True Name of God translated into American English for me, a native American English speaker. It was revealed to me in my own tongue and I had zero problems reciting it; when I meditate upon its meaning[s], it moves me to tears. That's why it was given to me IN MY OWN LANGUAGE. Now in the unseen spirit realms, it is no doubt free of the limitations of earthly language rules of any kind and is potent beyond mere mortal understanding. Translated for limited usage among us fleshy humans, it is packaged in a bite-sized format so that its utterance does not shatter the skull of the few people throughout the ages blessed to have had the honor to speak it. Although, it wasn't lost on me that my wife neither heard me speak it aloud nor saw me speaking anything in that moment, so that means I only spoke it from an altered consciousness state. My 'spirit man' is able to "speak" the NAME, but not my physical form.

Anyway, this experience does not make me a

prophet of God. May the Lord thy God forgive those of you who foolishly keep insisting this is so. Obviously, it is NOT so, per the guidance of the revealed message. The *Age of the Prophets* is over; the canon of sacred scripture is closed nigh these 1,500 years. In this post-prophetic age, my gifts mark me only as a Companion of the Right Hand, if it be God's Will. I am a committed believer in the Supreme Creator of reality, fully submitted to my Divine Maker. We all can gain these same gifts of the spirit if we are so committed—if God Wills it!

I'm writing this out to let you know these things, O Reader, including this: I aim to use my gifts to aid my people, to do my best to get my specific ethnic group our Reparations and our economic inclusion into the protected wealth-building ownership class we deserve. My aim is to manage the affairs of my religion from within the frame work of political activism for the American Descendants of Slavery, both the ethnic group and the noble ADOS Advocacy Foundation. An attack upon them is an attack upon me. Victory for them is victory for me.

Evil doers beware! This is a new day. #ADOS is here and *"coming to get our check!"*

very respectfully,

Malang Flathill

Artist | Activist | Muslim | Master of the Name

End

About the Author

Muhammad Rasheed is a cartoonist, socio-political commentator and 'artivist' for the American Descendants of Slavery (ADOS) political unification movement. His research interests include the anti-racism and pro-Reparations struggles of the Black American former slave class, its ties to antitrust law and the rise of the Second Gilded Age, with its lineage-based, systemic racism effects.

M. Rasheed's recent artivism effort is Weapon of the People: DECODED, a Gag-A-Day political cartoon venture launched on 09 Apr 2018. In addition to the backlist of previous works, his website features philosophical dialogues with ideological opponents from which the artist is inspired to create his work.